The Fourth Beast
Is Donald Trump the Antichrist?

Lawrence R. Moelhauser

Text copyright © 2016 Lawrence R. Moelhauser
All Rights Reserved

Legal Disclaimer: No part of this book may be reproduced or transmitted in any form or by any means, electronic or mechanical, including photocopying, recording or by any information storage and retrieval system, without express written permission from the author.

The information provided within this book is for general informational and entertainment purposes only, and represents no attempt to intentionally harm, discredit, or defame any person, living or dead. The views expressed are those of the author, and do not necessarily reflect the teachings or dogma of any particular faith, religious body, or other organization. The information was gathered through careful personal research of events and ideas, and through extensive fact-checking to present as accurate a view as possible, with the understanding that it is for entertainment purposes only, and that facts and points of view are subject to change with the passage of time. While the author has tried to keep the information up to date, truthful, and correct, there are no representations, express or implied, about the completeness, accuracy, reliability, suitability or availability with respect to the information or related graphics contained in this book for any purpose. Any use of this information is at your own risk.

Cover images of Donald Trump (2011) and Nuclear Explosion courtesy Pixabay Image Library
Cover design copyright © Lawrence R. Moelhauser
Book design and layout by Lawrence R. Moelhauser

Library of Congress Cataloging in Publication Data
Lawrence R. Moelhauser
The Fourth Beast: Is Donald Trump the Antichrist?
by Lawrence R. Moelhauser
ISBN-13:978-1535406499
ISBN-10:1535406496

Heartfelt Dedication

This book is dedicated to the United States of America, still the greatest country on the face of Planet Earth, and to all Americans—native-born and immigrant—who, through their selfless words and actions, continue every day to make America great!

Table of Contents

Attributes of the Antichrist…1

Introduction: Behind the Rhetoric…5

Part One: A Boastful Mouth…17

A Little History Lesson…19

All Trump, All the Time…25

Long and Beautiful…27

Iran…Iran and I Lost…31

No Respect, No Service, No Comment…35

Perfect Only in His Own Eyes…39

He Will Crush and Devour His Victims…49

A Few More Boastful Gems…55

Part One Wrap-up…57

Part Two: A Rash and Deceitful King…61

A Self-Deluded Liar…63

The Art of the Deception…69

America is Already Great!...73

A House Built Upon the Sand...79

A Fatal Wound is Healed...83

Deceiving the American People...85

Liar, Liar, Pants on Fire...89

And So, At Parting...97

Appendix: Graphs and Charts...101

Sources and Attributions...113

About the Author...117

"In my vision at night I looked, and there before me was a fourth beast, terrifying and frightening and very powerful"
--Daniel 6:7

Attributes of the Antichrist

1. Larger, stronger, more imposing and terrifying compared to other politicians *"...look was more stout than his fellows."(KJV); "...larger in appearance than its associates"(NASB); "...looked more imposing than the others."(NIV) ; "...was more terrifying than any of the others."(TEV)*—Daniel 7:20

2. Stern or fierce faced *"A king shall arise, having fierce features" (NKJV); "...a king of fierce countenance" (KJV, AMP); "...sternfaced"(NIV); "...bold countenance" (RSV, Darby)*—Daniel 8:23

3. Generally different or unique amongst politicians *"...and he will be different from the previous ones."*—Daniel 7:24

4. A great unifier who effectively appeals to people across traditional lines of division; will be revered by all. *"...the whole earth was amazed and followed after the beast."*—Revelation 13:3

5. Allegorically represented as incomparable metallic beast, of which he is also the personification; term beast applied to both him and his kingdom. *"...a fourth beast, dreadful and terrifying and extremely strong; and it had large iron teeth. It devoured and crushed, and trampled down the remainder with its feet; and it was different from all the beasts that were before it, and it had ten horns."*—Daniel 7-8

6. Seeks total political control for his own glory; not democratic republic or anything really for the people *"...who opposes and exalts himself above every so-called god or object of worship, so that he takes his seat in the temple of God, displaying himself as being God."*—2 Thessalonians 2:4

7. Icon of earthly success *"...he will succeed in whatever he* *does."*—Daniel 8:24

8. Politically rises from sub-national leadership position, like a governor *"...another horn [a ruler], a little one, came up among them [ten other rulers]...And out of one of [the 10 horns] came forth a rather small horn which grew exceedingly great."*—Daniel 7:8, 11

9. Will be shrewd, cunning, deceitful, skilled in intrigue *"Because he is cunning, he will succeed in his deceitful ways. He will be proud of himself and destroy many people without warning. He will even defy the greatest King of all, but he will be destroyed without the use of any human power."*—Daniel 8:25

10. Empowered through others *"And his power will be mighty, but not by his own power..."*—Daniel 8:24

11. Stubborn, relentless, mega-ambitious visionary with far reaching goals.

12. Vicious, violent, cruel, lacks regard for life *"Because he is cunning, he will succeed in his deceitful ways. He will be proud of himself and destroy many people without warning. He will even defy the greatest King of all, but he will be destroyed without the use of any human power."*—Daniel 8:25

13. Extraordinarily proud and boastful *"...this horn [ruler] possessed...a mouth uttering great boasts...I kept looking because of the sound of the boastful words which the horn was speaking...that horn which had...a mouth uttering great boasts...he will magnify himself in his heart."*—Daniel 7:8, 11, 20; 8:25

14. Disdain for women. *"And he will show no regard for ...the desire of women...for he will magnify himself above them all."*—Daniel 11:37

15. Inwardly a godless megalomaniac *"...that horn [ruler] was waging war with the saints and overpowering them...he will speak out against the Most High and wear down the saints of the Highest One."*
"...it grew up to the host of heaven and caused some of the host and some of the stars to fall to the earth, and it trampled them down. It even magnified itself to be equal with the Commander of the host; and it removed the regular sacrifice from Him, and the place of His sanctuary was thrown down... the host will be given over to the horn along with the regular sacrifice; ...And he will magnify himself in his heart...He will even oppose the Prince of princes."—Daniel 7:21, 25; 8:10-11, 25

16. Mega-liar who actively opposes truth *"...[he] will fling truth to the ground... .A king will arise Insolent and skilled in intrigue. And through his shrewdness He will cause deceit to succeed by his influence."*—Daniel 8:11, 23, 25

17. Morally bankrupt hedonist

18. Allegorically represented as a conqueror on a white horse
"And I looked, and behold, a white horse, and he who sat on it had a bow; and a crown was given to him; and he went out conquering, and to conquer."—Revelation 6:2

19. Foreshadowed by historical types including King Saul, Nebuchadnezzar, Caesar, Hitler

20. Professing Christianity, empowered by False Prophets, Christian support *"I am afraid, lest as the serpent deceived Eve by his craftiness, your minds should be led astray from the simplicity and purity of devotion to Christ. For if one comes and preaches another Jesus whom we have not preached, or you receive a different spirit which you have not received, or a* *different gospel which you have not accepted, you bear this beautifully. For such men are false apostles, deceitful workers, disguising themselves as apostles of Christ. And no wonder, for even Satan disguises himself as an angel of light. Therefore it is not surprising if his servants also disguise themselves as servants of righteousness; whose end shall be according to their deeds."*—2 Corinthians 11:3-15

Introduction:
Behind the Rhetoric

"...a despicable person will arise, on whom the honor of kingship has not been conferred, but he will come in a time of tranquility and seize the kingdom by intrigue."—Daniel 11:21

"By smooth words he will turn to godlessness those who act wickedly toward the covenant, but the people who know their God will display strength and take action."—Daniel 11:32

"Then the king will do as he pleases, and he will exalt and magnify himself above every god and will speak monstrous things...and he will prosper until the indignation is finished, for that which is decreed will be done. He will show no regard for the gods of his fathers or for the desire of women, nor will he show regard for any other god; for he will magnify himself above them all."—Daniel 11:36-37

Antichrist:

The word alone conjures up images of a devil-horned being come to deceive and lead astray; a dark lord; an evil sorcerer who practices black magic and casts terrifying spells; or even the son of Satan himself. To Christians, the term has (or should have) a special dual meaning, deeper and more profound than the secular "Hollywood" interpretation, with which most of us are familiar. John tells us in his Epistles that anyone who does not confess that Jesus is the Christ, and does not acknowledge Him as the Savior of Mankind, is *an* antichrist.

> "*Many deceivers have gone out into the world, those who do not confess that Jesus Christ has come in the flesh; any such person is the deceiver and the antichrist!*"—2 John 1:7

This passage has often been misrepresented to imply that anyone who does not believe in Jesus Christ and His sacrifice for mankind is evil. The world is comprised of many faiths and religious organizations, many of whom do not acknowledge Jesus as the Savior. Does this mean they are wicked and evil? Not necessarily. The term *antichrist*, as an adjective, simply refers to someone who does not believe in Christ. There is nothing wrong with that, and, as Matthew admonishes us, we should not judge them. Having said that, antichrist (the adjective) certainly refers to anyone who, openly or covertly, fights against Christians and Christianity, as in the case of terrorism. The real danger comes when self-righteous individuals—who profess Christianity but whose hearts are far from God—attempt to deceive others by preaching falsehoods disguised as truths, in an attempt to amass a following.

Which brings us to the more important reference and the one that will be the focus of this book, that of *The Antichrist*, a proper noun referring to the one who will be revealed in the last days, and will confront Jesus at His Second Coming. Though the actual name *Antichrist* as a proper noun never actually appears as such in the Bible, we do find repeated references to T*he Lawless One* and *The Beast* to describe the one who will oppose God.

"Let no one deceive you in any way; for that day will not come unless the rebellion comes first and the lawless one is revealed, the one destined for destruction. He opposes and exalts himself above every so called god or object of worship, so that he takes his seat in the temple of God, declaring himself to be God."—2 Thessalonians 2:1-4

This is a very important and critical distinction, for there have been many political and religious leaders throughout history who could be classified as anti-Christian but who do not qualify as *The Antichrist*. The Prophet Daniel, however, clearly tells us that *The Antichrist* will not be revealed until well into the future—*the distant future* in fact.

"The vision of the evenings and mornings that has been given you is true, but seal up the vision, for it concerns the distant future."—Daniel 8:26

Warning! I am going to be up front and straight forward with you: the material in this book is controversial. I have no doubt it will raise the ire of radicals and extremists who espouse to the fascist rants of Republican Presidential candidate Mr. Donald Trump and have become, by choice, his loyal followers.

However, beyond just creating controversy and stirring up anger, I sincerely hope to get the conversation going and to get people—especially the well-meaning and good-hearted who have been mesmerized and deceived by Mr. Trump's silver-tongued rhetoric, and have been blindly led away from the truth by his clever lies and intrigue—to take a hard look at the darker side of the man with the yellow hair who is clueless about politics, foreign policy, and religion, yet somehow fancies himself as our next President. More to the point, if you are one of the so-called *Trumpeteers* (a follower of *The Donald*) then I hope this book does, in fact, make you angry; because only by first getting angry will you be motivated to seek out the truth for yourself. Be very careful, however, that you temper that anger with reason and clear-headedness, so as not to allow your emotions to drive you to violent and illegal actions.

It is dangerous to take anything on blind faith, in particular the lies that politicians spout from the national stage. Though this book focuses on the underlying and sinister plan of Mr. Donald Trump—supported with eye-opening Biblical references—it also implies a greater and far-reaching warning never to take any politician at their word. They all use lies and half-truths to manipulate the emotions of the voting public in hopes of swaying them to their way of thinking. Make no mistake: it's a given in

American politics that most Americans make voting decisions based in large part on their emotions—spurred on by the news media's incessant stream of emotionally charged reporting—rather than on intelligent, thoughtful, and thorough research and study. Though important in the decision-making process, unbridled emotion not tempered by careful and objective study of all the issues – both left and right – can cause us to make bad decisions.

I am a registered Democrat, but that doesn't mean I agree with everything that Democrats say or do. I served for twenty-two years with the Federal Government, nearly half of that time as an Army Chaplain Assistant, so some of my political views lean decidedly to the Right. Some of my more personal belief systems have found a home in the more centric political realms of the Independent and Libertarian platforms. I have voted Republican, I've voted Green Party, and I've voted Democrat; and the possibility exists that I could vote differently again this November. This is because I try to look at the issues, and make my voting decisions based on how the majority of what the candidates are promising line up with what I believe to be best not only for myself, but for the country as a whole.

I would venture a guess, because of the emotion factor of politics, or because of peer pressure or the influence of family on political choice, that many of you may not be siding with the candidate you most align with, from a philosophical perspective. I found a great website recently, www.isidewith.com, where you can take a short survey, and based on the results of that survey, the site tells you which current candidate you most identify with, and how you stack up, percentage wise, with the other candidates. As suspected, Secretary Clinton is, in fact, the candidate I most identify with. I was surprised, however, to learn that 26% of my beliefs actually support Donald Trump's agenda. Does that mean I will change the way I feel about those particular issues? Of course not! The beliefs I feel most strongly about have shaped who I have become. This is true for all of us, and unless acting on those belief systems causes harm to you or to those around you, then there is no need to change them.

Donald Trump, of course, has mastered the art of emotional manipulation and exploits that weakness every chance he gets, stirring up the Republican base—and the country—at a purely emotional level. He is no idiot. He did not get to be a multi-millionaire by being stupid. He knows exactly what he's doing. He knows if he can get people emotionally riled up, by spouting lies and rhetoric and side-stepping the real issues, they will blindly follow him based on the way they *feel* about what he is saying. To illustrate this further, a few days after the terrorist attacks in Paris and in San Bernardino, I was engaged in a friendly debate with a young lady who supports Mr. Trump. The end of the conversation went something like this:

"*But, he doesn't address the issues facing Americans,*" I contended. "*And he certainly has no foreign policy agenda.*"

"*Of course he does,*" she argued. "*His foreign policy is 'let's blow them all to Hell*!'"

I chuckled and returned to my writing.

Clearly, this young lady's response was an emotional one, no doubt born out of those recent attacks. And who can blame her. Most Americans, including me, felt the same way right after the attacks of September 11th, 2001. *"Let's blow them all to Hell!"* But, that is pure rhetoric and should never be the foreign policy agenda of the President of the United States. It is interesting to note that Mr. Trump will often hold his campaign rallies—either coincidentally or by design—in areas of the country where the demographics lean predominantly towards the very ethnic groups he so vehemently rants against. His presence invariably invokes largely peaceful protests—a constitutional right—by members of those ethnicities. He then sends out his supporters to confront the protesters, stirring them up, and inciting a wild frenzy of verbal barbs and flying fists. He can then point to the chaos on the streets as supporting evidence that what he's saying must be true.

"A gentle answer turns away wrath, but a harsh word stirs up anger. A hot-tempered man stirs up strife, but the slow to anger calms a dispute."—Proverbs 15:1, 18

At the end of the day, though, a careful analysis of Mr. Trump's words reveals contradictions, insults, lack of knowledge on key and important issues, and a blatant disregard for anyone or anything contrary to his own bias. Even worse, what he says has little if any substance and fails to address the issues head on.

P.T. Barnum, co-founder of what is arguably the most successful circus in the world, once famously said: *"there's a sucker born every minute."* Like Barnum, Trump appears to be little more than the ring leader of his own personal circus. He's a showman—a reality TV star—performing for a willing and gullible audience, surrounding himself with hordes of screaming, loyal, fans, and ostracizing anyone who disagrees with his perverse sexist and racist agenda. He boasts about his wealth—as if anyone cares—and gloats about the many women he's slept with. He has embraced Barnum's *sucker principle* and exploits it for his own personal gain. He himself has unapologetically invoked Barnum's quote on occasion; as a means to his own narcissistic end.

This book represents my personal view of why I believe Donald Trump to be the best candidate to date, to qualify as *The Antichrist*. Through extensive research and careful interpretation of Biblical references to *"The Beast"*, specifically the books of *Daniel* and *Revelation*, which contain most of the details on how to recognize *The Antichrist*, I will attempt to uncover the sinister and frightening plot I believe to be lurking covertly behind Mr. Trump's gusher of narcissistic rhetoric.

I've found, as I have scoured the internet for information, that there are many political and religious views on how to identify *The Antichrist*. Some views are deeply rooted in Biblical prophecy and make a concerted effort to stay true to the presenter's religious dogma, while others are little more than the political rants of individuals with their own axe to grind, who really have no insight into the allegorical visions portrayed in the Bible, and erroneously try to pin the mantle of *antichrist* on political or religious leaders they simply don't like.

This is pure ignorance.

I will use as my primary resources Mr. Phil Maxwell's blog

post *"21 Attributes of the Antichrist"* on the *Yuku.com* forum *Simple Truth Discussion Center*; the non-partisan fact-check website, *PolitiFact.com*; experts in the fields of political science and psychology; and of course scriptural references from the Bible as the basis for my own conclusions and how I have attributed them to the presumptive Republican nominee, Mr. Donald Trump. I will also occasionally throw in a few personal anecdotes as flavor enhancers. After all, no one likes a bland steak!

Mr. Maxwell's blog post succinctly categorizes the attributes of *The Antichrist* and backs them up with scriptural references from multiple versions of the Bible. The attributes are a real eye-opener when compared with the volatile and divisive climate of this year's election cycle. His conclusions, posted years before Mr. Trump ever announced his intention to run for President, do not call out any specific individual as a potential Antichrist, but simply put the Biblical references into easy to understand bullet points, which we will explore in detail in the pages that follow. But, he does conclude, and rightly so, that *The Antichrist*, whoever he is, will come to political power in the *end times* and usher in the *Second Coming*.

Below are a few of the characteristics Mr. Maxwell has pulled together along with the scriptural reference. According to Mr. Maxwell's research, *The Antichrist* will be…

1. Larger, stronger, more imposing and terrifying physique compared to other politicians. (Daniel 7:20)

2. Stern or fierce faced. (Daniel 8:23)

3. Generally different or unique amongst politicians. (Daniel 7:24)

4. A great unifier who effectively appeals to people across traditional lines of division (Revelation 13:3)

5. Seeks total political control for his own glory; not democratic, republican or anything really for the people. (2 Thessalonians 2:4)

6. Icon of earthly success. (Daniel 8:24)

7. Will be shrewd, cunning, deceitful, skilled in intrigue. (Daniel 8:25)

While these qualities could apply to a number of world leaders, both current and past, I can think of no one currently on the world political stage, other than Mr. Trump, that so perfectly embodies all of them.

Most importantly, though, it is my intention to issue a wake-up call to Christians everywhere, who have been pulled off course by Mr. Trump's silver tongue. The Bible tells us that…

"…there shall arise false Christs, and false prophets, and shall show great signs and wonders; so that, if it were possible, they shall deceive the very elect."—Matthew 24:23-24

Do you hear what Jesus is telling you? He warns that many, even God's chosen ones, shall be drawn away from the truth by the words of *The Antichrist*. It never ceases to astound me how many God-fearing Christians in this country—normally kind, caring individuals—have thrown their support behind Mr. Trump and his message of hate and misogyny. As a result, they have become hateful, bigoted, and aggressive individuals themselves, taking literally Mr. Trump's advice to punch the protesters at his rallies "*in the face!*" These are not Christian values, my friends, and we should not fall prey to them. Mr. Trump is as far from the Christian tenants of kindness, loving one another, and treating others as we wish to be treated, as one can get. We are warned about this in scripture, where we are told that the evil one shall appear as an angel of light, and that many will be compelled to follow him. Indeed, *The Antichrist* follows a very different master than the one Christians should follow and emulate.

There is no doubt that Donald Trump exudes a charismatic personality that is appealing to many, mostly because he verbalizes what many would like to say out loud, but know they cannot, because the filters of a civilized community remind us that it is foolhardy to say whatever pops into our brains. So instead, many use Mr. Trump as a surrogate mouthpiece of hateful, mean-spirited rhetoric, allowing him to say all the things they wish they could. Do not be deceived by this man's evil agenda, dear friends. Steer clear of his path. Do not be over-come by his boastful words and his lies.

As you read this book, I urge you to do so with an open mind, and then go out and conduct your own research and study, and find out for yourselves if the conclusions I've arrived at make sense, or if I'm completely off base. I don't expect everyone to agree with me. In fact, I expect vehement opposition. That is a good thing, because only by realizing how the prophecies regarding *The*

Antichrist are unfolding before our eyes, will we be more vigilant and prepared when the storms do arise.

Part One:
A Boastful Mouth

"...there before me was another horn, a little one, which came up among them...This horn had eyes like the eyes of a man and a mouth that spoke boastfully. Then I continued to watch because of the boastful words the horn was speaking. I also wanted to know about the ten horns on [the forth beast's]head and about the other horn that came up...the horn that looked more imposing than the others and that had eyes and a mouth that spoke boastfully."—Daniel 7:8, 11, 20 (NIV)

"He gave me this explanation: 'The fourth beast is a fourth kingdom that will appear on earth. It will be different from all the other kingdoms and will devour the whole earth, trampling it down and crushing it. The ten horns are ten kings who will come from this kingdom. After them another king will arise, different from the earlier ones... He will speak against the Most High and oppress his holy people and try to change the set times and the laws. The holy people will be delivered into his hands for [a year, two years, and a half a year]."—Daniel 7:23-25 (NIV)

A Little History Lesson

In his vision of the four beasts in the passages above, the Prophet Daniel gives us a clear picture of the physical attributes of *The Antichrist*.

Most Bible scholars and theologians agree that the four beasts of which Daniel spoke refer to the four major ruling empires of that time period: The Chaldean Empire, which comprised modern-day Iraq, Syria, and parts of Turkey; The Medo-Persian Empire, controlled by the Medes and the Persians, of whom Daniel prophesied would overthrow the Kingdom of Babylon (*Daniel 5:30-31*); The Greek Empire; and finally The Roman Empire (or, by some accounts, the United States). But, here's where things get a bit murky. There seems to be no clear consensus on what the ten horns that arise from the *fourth beast* represent, and even less on "*the little horn, which came up among them...*" Some accounts describe the ten horns as ten revival periods following the fall of the Roman Empire, and the little horn as a nebulous religious organization designated to usher in the Second Coming of Jesus. Other accounts are a bit more consistent and concrete, believing the horns represent major rulers through time, and that the little horn is either a descendent (by some accounts) of one of the major rulers, or *a minor political figure who rises quickly to power*. I am inclined to go with the latter interpretation, with one major caveat. I believe, through my research, that the fourth beast is not the Roman Empire, but that Daniel, in his vision, was witnessing the fracturing of Israel and the dispersal of the *Ten "Lost" Tribes*.

"For I will give the command, and I will shake the people of Israel among all the nations as grain is shaken in a sieve..."— Amos 9:9

If we look at the map below **(figure 1)**, we see that many of the tribes settled throughout mainland Europe after being *shaken out* of Israel.

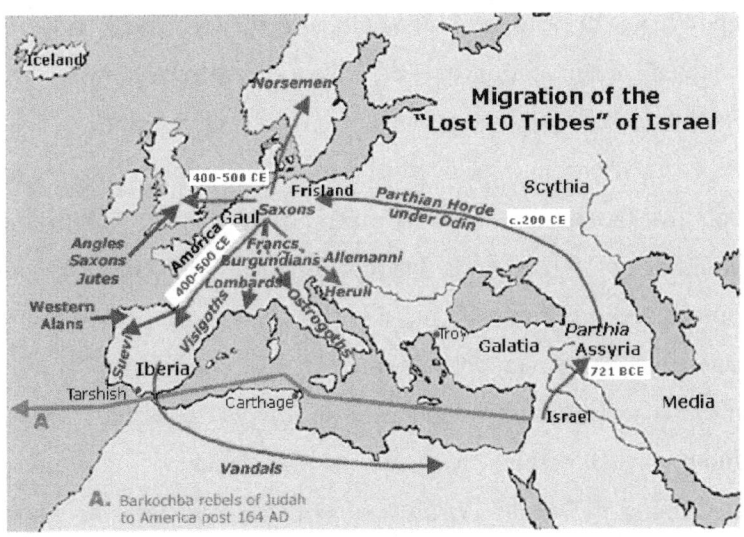

Figure 1: The "shaking" of the people of Israel among all nations

So, how does all of this relate to Donald Trump? I'm so glad you asked.

Frederick Christ Trump, grandfather of Donald Trump, was born on March 14th, 1869 in Kallstadt, Rheinland-Pfalz, Germany. He immigrated in 1885 to the United States from Hamburg aboard the ship "Eider" and became a U.S. citizen in 1892 in Seattle, Washington. He began his fortune running the

Arctic Restaurant and Hotel in Bennett, British Columbia, during the Klondike Gold Rush.

Of course, this in and of itself means nothing – my own parents emigrated from Germany after World War II – until we start putting all the pieces together. Since Daniel gives no clear timeline as to exactly when the *little horn* would rise up, we can speculate. Assuming that Daniel is saying *The Antichrist* will come to power just prior to the Second Coming, we can already rule out tyrannical leaders from world history, such as Hitler and Mussolini, both of whom have been cast in the role of *The Antichrist* at one time or another throughout history. There is no doubt that these men, and many others, have certainly fulfilled the definition of *an antichrist*, but not as *The Antichrist*, of whom Daniel spoke. Additionally, up until now, no single person to my knowledge has so completely met all the criteria set forth in scripture as to the definition of *The Antichrist*, as has Donald Trump; which brings us back to the focus of this book: determining if Donald Trump could be *The Antichrist* of whom Daniel spoke.

The German people are keenly aware of Mr. Trump's ancestry and his connection to the city of Kallstadt. So much so, in fact, that the German periodical *Die Welt* (The World) published an article on August 24th, 2015, titled *Donald Trump: King of Kallstadt*. The article featured a one-sheet movie poster, advertising German documentarian, Simone Wendel's, 2014 release "Kings of Kallstadt", a farcical look at Mr. Trump's family history. Mr. Trump's face is displayed prominently in the center of the poster, designating him as *the king*. **(See Figure 2.)**

It's interesting to note that the German people refer to Donald Trump, and to his ancestors, as "kings". What was it the Prophet Daniel said about *The Antichrist*?

> "*The ten horns **are ten kings** who will come from this kingdom. After them **another king** will arise, different from the earlier ones... He will speak against the Most High and oppress his holy people and try to change the set times and the laws.*"—Daniel 7:24-25 (emphasis added)

We will explore the above passage in more detail later in this section, but for the moment, give these points some prayerful consideration. Is Mr. Trump *different from the earlier* "kings" and from current political figures? I would say so. Does Mr. Trump—whether intentionally or not—*speak against the Most High*? He mocks God, he mocks the Holy Communion, and he mocks The Bible, so I would say yes. Is Mr. Trump trying *to change set times and the laws*? Every chance he gets, he boasts about the many laws and policies he wants to change or repeal if he becomes President; many of which have been in place for decades and have become the foundation of this country's political and legal system. He rants about the walls he will build and about mass deportations of entire ethnic groups. Judging from his campaign rhetoric, it seems to me that his intent is to change everything he can to satisfy his own narcissism and low self-esteem.

Coincidence? Perhaps. Still, when you put all the pieces together, it's easy to see how Daniel's vision clearly delineates what is happening right now in our country, on the vast political stage, and the negative impact Mr. Trump's candidacy is having on this country, and on the world as a whole.

Figure 2: Theater One Sheet © 2014 Simone Wendel

All Trump, All the Time

There is little question that Donald Trump possesses an arrogant and boastful disposition. Indeed, never in the history of US Presidential politics has there ever been a candidate who has displayed as much hubris, arrogance, and narcissism as Mr. Trump. With him, it seems to be his way or no way. Let's take a look at some examples.

According to a *Media Research Center* report covering CNN Prime Time weekday shows between August 24th, 2015 and September 4th, 2015, Donald Trump received 580 minutes of on air coverage, over 77% of the total air time given all seventeen GOP Candidates during that time period. His next closest rival, Jeb Bush, received only 88 total air-time minutes, or just fewer than 12%. Air time for the other fifteen candidates was negligible, at best. **(See Appendix, Figure 3.)**

According to my research, since beginning his campaign for the Presidency, Mr. Trump has held no less than 29 phone interviews with the major television networks—and I am sure there will be many more to follow—compared to the other candidates who've collectively conducted exactly zero phone "appearances". Rather than take the time to visit the show and be interviewed face to face, Trump claims phone interviews are more efficient since he can sit in the comfort of his home or office and conduct several interviews in one day. While this may be true from a business stand-point, it doesn't work for someone running for the highest office in the free world. His arrogance and hubris are the impetuses that drive these pompous decisions. To their credit, NBC and CBS have allegedly cut off Mr. Trump's phone privileges, and we can only hope more networks will follow suit.* During a September 2015 Campaign Rally in Dallas, Texas, Mr. Trump justified his domination of the airwaves this way:

> *"You know, on television, on FOX and CNN, they call it all Trump all the time. Can you believe it? All Trump all the time. And by the way, their ratings are through the roof. If they weren't, they wouldn't put me on. I'll be honest with you. It's a simple formula in entertainment and television. If you get good ratings — if you get good ratings — and these aren't good, these are monster — then you'll be on all the time, even if you have nothing to say...."* (Trump; Dallas, Texas; December, 2015)

---

*The networks' "call-in" embargo against Mr. Trump is apparently working. In recent weeks he has been appearing in person far more frequently and conducting far fewer phone interviews.

Long and Beautiful

Though still boastful and narcissistic in an extreme way, not everything *The Donald* brags about is coupled with dire consequences. Some of it is actually hilarious, if only in a juvenile, school-yard, sort of way. I'm sure we all remember the February 25th, 2016 GOP debate during which Senator Marco Rubio commented on the size of Donald Trump's hands, implying that since he has small hands, other parts of his anatomy must be small as well. While I believe Mr. Rubio was out of line, embarrassing not only himself and his supporters, but his family as well, and that he committed political suicide by those remarks, it's telling to note how Mr. Trump responded. Observe:

"Look at those hands, are they small hands? And, Marco Rubio referred to my hands: 'If they're small, something else must be small.' I guarantee you there's no problem. I guarantee." (Trump; February 25th, 2016; GOP Presidential Debate)

But apparently this is not the first time Mr. Trump has been overly-obsessed with the size of his hands and the implication thereof. For the past 25 years, Mr. Trump has been allegedly sending photographs of his hands and fingers – often circled with gold Sharpie® for added emphasis – to *Vanity Fair* editor Graydon Carter, in an effort to prove his fingers are properly proportioned. The decades-long finger-feud began when Carter wrote an article for *Spy* magazine allegedly referring to Mr. Trump as a *"short-fingered vulgarian"*. Of the ongoing deluge of "hand mail", Mr. Carter made the following observation in the Editor's Letter of the

October 2015 issue of *Vanity Fair*:

> "*The most recent offering arrived earlier this year, before his decision to go after the Republican presidential nomination. Like the other packages, this one included a circled hand and the words, also written in gold Sharpie: 'See, not so short!' I sent the picture back by return mail with a note attached, saying, 'Actually, quite short.'*" (Carter, Editor's Letter; Vanity Fair Magazine, Oct 2015)

As if that's not funny enough, per usual Trump demeanor when his ego is bruised, the spoiled, arrogant, rich brat from New York spat back in a Twitter® post.

> "*Rumor has it that the grubby head of failing @VanityFair Magazine, 'sloppy' Graydon Carter, is going to be fired or replaced very soon?*" (Twitter; @realDonaldTrump, 16 October, 2015, 2:33pm)

Yes, the tweet really did end with a question mark, which makes me wonder if Mr. Trump is really as smart as he thinks; just another example of his boastful mouth.

Apparently Mr. Carter's comments really cut Donald Trump to the quick. In 2011 he felt compelled to take his finger-defense further when he told *Page Six* of the New York Post:

> "*My fingers are long and beautiful, as it has been well documented, are various other parts of my body.*" (Trump; New York Post *Page Six* interview; 2011)

The long and short of it, Mr. Carter was right: Donald Trump is indeed vulgar. This would all be laughable except for the fact that Mr. Trump was not joking. To him, this was a serious matter that needed to be dealt with, and he was determined to get his way, no matter what the cost; which makes his run for the US Presidency all the more frightening.

Now back to more serious and dangerous examples of Donald Trump's *"mouth that spoke boastfully"*

Iran...Iran and I Lost

"*So I've been doing deals for a long time. I've been making lots of wonderful deals, great deals. That's what I do. Never, ever, ever in my life have I seen any transaction so incompetently negotiated as our deal with Iran. And I mean never. If I win the Presidency, I guarantee you that those four prisoners are back in our country before I ever take office. They will be back before I ever take office, because they (the Iranians) know that's what has to happen, O.K.? They know it. And if they don't know it, I'm telling them right now.*" (Donald Trump; September 2015; Outside the US Capitol Bldg; Washington, D.C.)

What makes this so incredibly arrogant and bombastic is that there has never, in the history of this country, been a hostage release negotiated that has not taken years, working through many channels in many countries, to be successful. Mr. Trump seems to be saying that he can just tell the Iranians to release the hostages and they will comply.

Talk about hubris!

The release of Mr. Terry Anderson, who was taken hostage by Hezbollah in 1985 while working as the Associated Press Bureau Chief in Beirut, and who has been the longest held American hostage to date, took seven years and spanned two Presidencies. Mr. Anderson had this to say about Donald Trump's Iran hostage solution:

"*It doesn't make sense. The Iranians aren't at Trump's beck-and-call, and they won't be if he's elected President. It's so idiotic that I don't know how to address it.*

One of the first things a President learns when he comes into office is that he can't simply order things and make them happen—in our government, let alone anyone else's." (Anderson, US Hostage, held in Iran 1985-1991, from *The New Yorker*; Sept 11th, 2015)

Congressman Dan Kildee (D - Michigan), who in the summer of 2015 won unanimous, bipartisan support in the US House of Representatives for a proposed resolution on Americans held hostages in Iran, made this observation regarding Mr. Trump's boastful nature:

"It's not the loudest voice or the most caustic language that gets things done, whether in domestic policy or international relations. It takes more than holding the microphone to actually make progress in this country. Name-calling should not have a place in American political space—especially in a subject as sensitive as Iran nuclear negotiations or the status of Americans held against their will." (Kildee, US Congressman, 2015)

It is painfully clear that Donald Trump knows nothing about foreign policy. But, rather than admit he doesn't know and that he will research the subject and learn, he puffs himself up like a blow fish and boats how he will be able to immediately bring the world to the negotiating table to do his bidding. There is no doubt that Mr. Trump is an incredibly successful businessman who clearly has mastered the *Art of the Deal*, and is probably the best business negotiator this country has seen in decades. When it comes to business, he is a veritable *Wunderkind*. But, business tactics do not work when it comes to foreign policy. To arrogantly believe the

Iranian leaders will bow to his desires simply because he tells them they should is not only delusional but downright dangerous! I don't think Mr. Trump fully understands the ramifications of such an attempt, and the proverbial *Pandora's Box* he would be opening. It is frightening!

No Respect; No Service; No Comment

In the summer of 2015, speaking at the Family Leadership Summit in Ames, Iowa, Donald Trump wasted no time shoving his foot deep into his mouth again. His now famous remarks regarding Senator John McCain's (R-Arizona) capture and subsequent torture as a POW in North Vietnam unleashed a twitter storm that continues to this day.

"He's not a war hero. He was a war hero because he was captured. I like people who weren't captured." (Trump; Family Leadership Summit; Ames, Iowa; July 18th, 2015)

As is his *modus operandi*, Mr. Trump only tells half the truth here and even that he artfully twists to serve his own selfish needs and desires, always turning it back towards his arrogant self. You see, Mr. Trump is actually partly correct: Senator McCain is not a war hero *because* he was captured, he's a war hero because of what he did *while* in captivity. Shortly after Senator McCain's imprisonment at the *Hanoi Hilton*, his captors gave him an opportunity for freedom, ostensibly because of Mr. McCain's familial connections to the US Navy's Fleet Admiralty, but

McCain refused to leave. When asked why, he said he was living by a sacred military code and that he would not abandon his fellow servicemen, who were also in captivity with him. The North Vietnamese then tried a different tack, saying they had orders from then U.S. President Lyndon Johnson to release him and send him home immediately.

What Senator McCain did not know is that there were no such orders, just the same he stood by his word and again refused to leave Vietnam. As a consequence of this choice, Senator McCain endured over five years of torturous captivity, two of which were in solitary confinement. His resolve to stand by "the code", even knowing it could mean his death, is what makes Senator McCain a war hero, a fact Mr. Trump seems to care very little about.

The backlash from Mr. Trump's fellow Republicans was swift and appropriate:

"*Enough with the slanderous attacks,*" *Jeb Bush tweeted. "@SenJohnMcCain and all our veterans - particularly POWs have earned our respect and admiration.*"

"*John McCain is an American hero. I have nothing but respect for his service to our country,*" *tweeted Louisiana Gov. Bobby Jindal. "After Donald Trump spends six years in a POW camp, he can weigh in on John McCain's service.*"

"*@SenJohnMcCain is an American hero & all POW's deserve our nation's highest debt of gratitude. @realDonaldTrump's comments are disgraceful,*" *tweeted former Texas Gov. Rick Perry. "As a fellow veteran I respect @SenJohnMcCain because he volunteered to serve his country. I cannot say the same about Mr. @realDonaldTrump.*"

South Carolina Sen. Lindsey Graham, a close friend of McCain's, tweeted, "If there was ever any doubt that @realDonaldTrump should not be our commander in chief, this stupid statement should end all doubt." He added: "At the heart of @realDonaldTrump statement is a lack of respect for those who have served - a disqualifying characteristic to be president."

As an Army Veteran myself, I find Donald Trump's lack of respect for the men and women who serve in the armed forces offensive.

This from a man who received no less than *four* student deferments from military service between 1964 and 1968, and a medical deferment after graduating for an alleged bone spur in his foot. To me, these are the actions of a coward!

Donald Trump's lack of respect for the military and the brave, selfless men and women who serve this great country, has even turned Republican establishment hard-liners against him. This man's *boastful mouth* is alienating his fellow Republicans, our allies around the globe, and humankind in general. Not only that, his toxic rhetoric is strengthening the resolve of our enemies, rather than breaking it down as he so arrogantly declares. Whether or not he chooses to believe it, his scorched earth approach to foreign policy and his messages of hate towards anyone who opposes him or his ideas, are actually helping terrorist organizations such as *ISIS*. He has, in effect, become their favorite and most active recruiter.

"It will be different from all the other kingdoms and will devour the whole earth, trampling it down and crushing it."— Daniel 7:23

Perfect Only in His Own Eyes

"...a stern-faced king, a master of intrigue, will arise. He will become very strong, but not by his own power. He will cause astounding devastation and will succeed in whatever he does. He will destroy the mighty men and the holy people. He will...consider himself superior. When they feel secure, he will destroy many and take his stand against the Prince of Princes. The vision...that has been given you is true, but seal up the vision for it concerns the distant future."—Daniel 8:23-26 (NIV)

"The king will do as he pleases. He will exalt and magnify himself above every god and will say unheard of things...He will be successful until the time of wrath is completed. He will show no regard for the gods of his fathers or for the one desired by women...but will exalt himself above them all. Instead of them, he will honor a god of fortresses...he will honor with gold and silver, with precious stones and costly gifts."—Daniel 11:36-38 (NIV)

There is a lot of material in Daniel's vision regarding the hateful and arrogant nature of *The Antichrist*, and how he will see himself as being above everyone, even God. Daniel also speaks to the godlessness of *The Antichrist*, even though he will present himself as being a believer and a good Christian. However, when the wolf finally emerges from under his sheep skin exterior, the real enemy will be revealed. As I pointed out in my opening paragraphs, many Bible scholars believe Daniel's vision dealt with what was happening in the world during his time, but we can see, very definitively in Chapter 8, verse 26 that this was not the case at all. God instructed Daniel to *"seal up the vision for it concerns **the distant future**"* (emphasis added).

It is frightening, and illuminating at the same time, how

Donald Trump fulfills Daniel's prophesy almost to the letter. His message of hate seems to be a continual stream of misogynistic and racist remarks against women, Muslims, Mexicans, Jews, and pretty much anyone else who doesn't look or think like him, including members of his own party. From throwing peaceful protestors from his rallies (so much for upholding the First Amendment) to insisting he will make the Mexicans pay for a Southern Border wall, to denigrating women, he makes all those who have preceded him seem mild by comparison.

Mr. Trump likes to wave the *Holy Bible* in front of his followers at his rallies, claiming that he is a God-loving, church-going Christian, and that he loves The Bible and knows its teachings. Nothing could be further from the truth.

At the 2015 Family Leadership Summit in Ames, Iowa Mr. Trump was asked by the moderator if he had ever sought God's forgiveness. Mr. Trump's reply is further evidence of his boastful and arrogant nature:

"I'm not sure I have ever asked God's forgiveness. I don't bring God into that picture." (Trump; Family Leadership Summit; Ames, Iowa; July 18th, 2015)

In an act of artful back-peddling, Mr. Trump then attempted to justify his comment by clarifying what to him constitutes forgiveness:

"When I go to church and when I drink my little wine and have my little cracker, I guess that is a form of forgiveness. I do that as often as I can because I feel cleansed. I say let's go on and let's make it right," (Ibid.)

When asked in a follow-up question if asking for forgiveness was an important tenant of his faith, Donald Trump, in his usual smug, pompous demeanour replied:

"I try not to make mistakes where I have to ask forgiveness. Why do I have to repent, or ask for forgiveness, if I'm not making mistakes?"(Trump; *Anderson Cooper 360*; July 2015)

Well, I'll tell you why, Donald: because the Bible tells us that no one is perfect, and that we have all sinned and fallen short of God's glory (Romans 3:10, 23). Do you see yourself as so righteous that you are incapable of sin? There is only one man I know of, in the history of the world, who was completely without sin, and—news flash—his name is *not* Trump.

Daniel tells us that *The Antichrist* will see himself as a god, sinless and without the need to repent. Additionally, in his second letter to the Thessalonians, the apostle Paul tells us that *The Antichrist* will be one

"...who will oppose and will exalt himself above everything that is called God or is worshiped, so that he sets himself up in God's temple (the church), *proclaiming himself to be God."*—2 Thessalonians 2: 4 (NIV)

By saying he has no reason to ask God for forgiveness, because he does not make mistakes, Mr. Trump is, in effect, implying that he is as sinless as only Jesus was, and that therefore he is god-like, unequivocally fulfilling Paul's prophesy that *The Antichrist* will proclaim *"himself to be God."*

In a later interview, while talking about his appearance in

Iowa, Mr. Trump left us with this telling remark, effectively distilling the sacred sacraments of the Holy Communion down to a joke:

"We were having fun when I said I drink the wine, I eat the cracker. The whole room was laughing." (Trump; *Anderson Cooper 360*; July 2015)

Once again we see evidence of the divine prophecies of Daniel fulfilled through Mr. Trump's bombastic, boastful behavior:

"...will speak out against the Most High, and wear down the saints of the Highest One...and it removed the regular sacrifice (represented by the Holy Communion) *from Him, and the place of His sanctuary was thrown down... the host will be given over to the horn along with the regular sacrifice; ...and he will magnify himself in his heart...He will even oppose the Prince of Princes."*—Daniel 7:21, 25; 8:10-11, 25

The main reason I began this section with Mr. Trump's views on forgiveness and repentance, is because they speak to the very heart from where his bigotry and hatred stem.

Any man who sees himself as sinless and perfect, never making mistakes, and as one who has no need for God's grace and forgiveness, is free to do and say anything he pleases, to whomever he pleases, on any topic he pleases. Since in his own eyes he has achieved perfection, then what he says must be true, and the rest of imperfect humanity must listen to what he says and follow his way. If this does not fall under the classification of false prophet, then nothing does.

Since we've established the well-spring from which Donald Trump's bigotry and hatred flow, let us take a closer look at some his more frightening and misogynistic attacks towards those who do not think or look or act as he thinks they should.

"These people come near to me with their mouth and honor me with their lips, but their hearts are far from me. Their worship of me is based on merely human rules they have been taught."— Isaiah 29:13

Mr. Trump's school-girl fixation on all things inconsequential is nothing new. During the October 2012 Presidential Debates between President Obama and challenger Mitt Romney, Donald Trump seemed unnaturally obsessed with the on-again off-again relationship between *Twilight* co-stars Robert Pattinson and Kristen Stewart. Here are a couple of examples from what became a two-month twitter explosion:

"*Robert Pattinson should not take back Kristen Stewart. She cheated on him like a dog and will do it again; just watch. He can do much better.*" (Twitter;@realDonaldTrump, Oct 2012)

"*Everyone knows I am right that Robert Pattinson should dump Kristen Stewart. In a couple of years, he will thank me. Be smart, Robert.*" (Twitter; @realDonaldTrump, Oct 2012)

As someone who has claims to be keenly interested in the "important" issues that Americans face, and that it's time for a change in Washington DC, Mr. Trump spends most of his energy focused on skirting around the issues, instead of facing them head on. Rather than pay attention to the Presidential Debate, and perhaps learn something worthwhile in the process, he chose to focus on his hypocritical concern for a television star's lack of fidelity. Mr. Trump is certainly not blameless in issues of monogamy. He brags about all the women he has slept with over the years, including married women. Worse yet, he has actually said he would *"probably be dating"* Ivanka if she weren't his daughter! This brings us back again to Mr. Trump's assertion that he is a good Christian and that he never makes mistakes that require God's forgiveness. How can he be a so without sin, yet continually violate the basic principles that Christians around the world hold so dear.

"You have heard it said, 'Love your neighbor and hate your enemy.' But I tell you: love your enemies, and pray for those who persecute you."—Matthew 6:43-44 (NIV)

Here are a few more of Mr. Trump's childish, unimportant rants:

"Arianna Huffington is unattractive, both inside and out. I fully understand why her former husband left her for a man. He made a good decision." (Twitter; @realDonaldTrump; August 2012)

In one statement, Mr. Trump manages to not only insult Ms Huffington—one of the most successful women in media—but also seems to be advocating gay rights; an issue on which he has continually flip-flopped, depending on his mood and the audience he is addressing.

"You know, it really doesn't matter what the media write as long as you've got a young and beautiful piece of ass." (From an interview with *Esquire*; 1991)

This is almost laughable because, if you didn't understand the insulting colloquialism *piece of ass*, you might infer—as perhaps many non-English speakers did—that he's talking about his own ass! Unfortunately, this comment is no laughing matter. He may think his disparaging remarks are funny, but in reality they again illustrate Mr. Trump's penchant for childish, frat-boy, beer-hall "humor" that most self-respecting women would find offensive and off-putting. I personally know of no woman who enjoys being referred to as an object to be used and discarded.

"If I were running The View, I'd fire Rosie O'Donnell. I mean, I'd look at her right in that fat, ugly face of hers, I'd say "Rosie, you're fired!" (From *Entertainment Tonight*; 2006)

That there is an on-going feud between Donald Trump and Rosie O'Donnell is no secret. However, what Mr. Trump does not seem to understand is that you can disagree with someone's point of view, and you can rebut statements they make about your character or your lack of ability to lead a nation, but you do it on a civilized level and don't resort to juvenile, school-yard name-calling. But juvenile tactics seem to be Mr. Trump's stock in trade. Is that what they teach you in business school, Donald: when someone disagrees with you call them foul names, make fun of their looks, attack who they are, and you're sure to win the negotiation? Somehow I doubt it. That seems to only hold true in the *Donald Trump School of Disarming your Enemies Through the use of Childish Temper Tantrums.* Thankfully there is no such school (There's one that comes close – *Trump University* – but let's save that for the next section on Trump's masterful deception tactics).

"*If Hillary Clinton can't satisfy her husband, what makes her think she can satisfy America?*" (Twitter; @realDonaldTrump; April 16th, 2015)

"[She had] *blood coming out of her eyes, blood coming out of her...wherever.*" –about Fox News journalist Megyn Kelly who had confronted him at a Republican debate over his sexist remarks regarding women.

The Prophet Daniel goes on to tell us this about *The Antichrist*:

"*Neither shall he regard the God of his fathers, **nor the desire of women**, nor regard any god: for he shall magnify himself above all.*"—Daniel 11:37 (Emphasis added)

"*The king will do as he pleases. He will exalt and magnify himself above every god and will say unheard of things...*"—Daniel 11:36

At this point, there should be little doubt that Donald Trump is fulfilling Biblical prophecy regarding *The Antichrist*, but since we still have a lot of ground to cover, let's continue on with some more examples.

Women are not the only members of society he has vehemently spoken out against with unfiltered impunity. His bigotry and his racist remarks towards Muslims and Mexicans have become infamous. Indeed, they bear a striking and frightening resemblance to comments made by Adolf Hitler nearly three-quarters of a century ago. And so, history repeats itself. Let's look at Mr. Trump's so called solutions to issues of immigration and terrorism and you decide for yourself if this doesn't sound like Daniel's description of *The Antichrist* when he prophesied:

"It [the beast] *will be different from all other kingdoms and will devour the whole earth, trampling it down and crushing it."*—Daniel 7:23

"He will cause astounding devastation and will succeed in whatever he does. He will destroy the mighty men and the holy people. He will...consider himself superior. When they [the people] *feel secure, he will destroy many..."*—Daniel 8:24-25

And what has Mr. Trump said that fulfills Daniel's vision?

"I will build a great wall – and nobody builds walls better than me, believe me – and I'll build them very inexpensively. I will build a great, great wall on our southern border, and I will make Mexico pay for that wall. Mark my words." (Trump; June 2015; Candidacy Announcement Speech)

Again, just like his assertion that he will make Iran release the American hostages, Mr. Trump thinks he can simply speak and the world will obey. How little he understands Foreign Policy and Diplomacy. He understands even less about the will of God. Moving on:

"When Mexico sends its people, they're not sending the best. They're not sending you; they're sending people that have lots of problems with us. They're bringing drugs. They're bringing crime. They're rapists." (ibid.)

"*They're* [the Muslims] *not coming to this country if I'm president. And if Obama has brought some to this country they are leaving, they're going, they're gone.*" (Trump; GOP Debate, December 2015, Las Vegas, NV)

He Will Crush and Devour His Victims

Beyond his blatant misogynistic and bigoted remarks, there is a more subtle yet far more insidious undercurrent to Donald Trump's meteoric rise on the political stage and to his aspirations: he seeks total political control, and he doesn't care how he gets it.

"The king will do as he pleases."—Daniel 11:36

For years, he has been flip-flopping on the important issues: first he's pro-choice, then he's pro-life; first he's for Syrian refugees entering the US, then he wants to deport them out of the country; first he's for a ban on assault weapons, then he opposes the ban; and so on. Now don't misunderstand me. There's nothing wrong with changing your mind. At the end of the day Presidential Candidates are only human and, like all of us, are entitled to change their minds and revisit issues from a different angle. But, when they change their position, they need to be transparent and humble enough to say they've reconsidered those issues and view them differently now. Mr. Trump does not do that. This gives the impression that he does not really know—or even care about—where he stands on the critical issues facing America today, and as such, does not identify with any particular political party. He's neither Democrat nor Republican, and he certainly doesn't identify with Independent voters either. Instead, he seeks total political control for his own glory, and not for the benefit of the people. Let's take another look at the Apostle Paul's second letter to the Thessalonians, in which he actually alluded to this characteristic of

The Antichrist:

"Don't let anyone deceive you in any way, for that day [the Second Coming of Jesus] *will not come until the rebellion occurs and the man of lawlessness is revealed, the man doomed to destruction. He will oppose...everything that is called God or is worshiped...proclaiming himself to be God. For the secret power of lawlessness is already at work; but the one who now holds it back* [President Obama] *will continue to do so till he is taken out of the way. And then the lawless one will be revealed."*—2 Thessalonians 2:3-4, 7-9

It's very clear Paul was writing about a time when a current leader would be *"holding back"* the powers of lawlessness that are about to be revealed. President Obama has put into place many laws and policies for the benefit of the American People that Mr. Trump can't wait to dismantle and *"trample underfoot."* Though Trump is already a formidable presence in the political arena, his hands are tied and his power limited until such time that President Obama leaves office at the end of this, his last term. The above passage seems to say, that even if Donald Trump is not actually elected President, he will still wield unprecedented power and influence over politics and policies that affect this country, and that he will attempt to use his celebrity status to stir things up. He's already threatened to sue or to incite his followers to violence at the Republican National Convention should he not become his party's nominee. Can you imagine what he would try to do if he is not then elected President?

Fortunately, the Apostle Paul also tells us that there will be a rebellion (riot, uprising, revolution) and that *"the man of lawlessness* [will be] *doomed to destruction."* (2 Thessalonians 2:3)

To drive the point home, look at the violence against protesters that have already occurred at Trump rallies across the country!

He has effectively alienated women voters by suggesting that he would make abortion illegal and then punish women who get an abortion. He has insulted our allies by wanting to pull out of NATO and by implying that we should use nuclear weapons against *ISIS*, advocating giving nuclear weapons to Japan, South Korea, and even to Saudi Arabia, yet all the while speaking out *against* the proliferation of nuclear weapons. Without actually saying it, Mr. Trump would like nothing better than for the United States to be the only country in the world allowed to possess a nuclear arsenal, thus ensuring he would have total control over the complete and utter destruction of any country that dare oppose him and his will.

"...terrifying and frightening, and very powerful. It had large, iron teeth; it crushed and devoured its victims and trampled underfoot whatever was left. A river of fire was flowing, coming out from before him."—Daniel 7:7, 10

Clearly, Mr. Trump can be categorically described as *frightening and very powerful*. The allegory that *The Antichrist* will have *large, iron teeth that crush and devour its victims* is painfully visible every time Mr. Trump opens his mouth. He never seems to focus on the issues a President would need to deal with, but rather chooses to engage in personal attacks against whomever he wishes, depending on how he feels at any given moment.

And you dare not say anything even remotely negative to or about him lest he unleash his wrath against you through caustic twitter feeds and from his *high horse* at debates and rallies.

But there is an even more frightening and sinister plot implied in Donald Trump's dangerous rhetoric. If we look closely at Daniel's vision, it's not a far stretch to infer he was seeing modern warfare at work. By today's standards, the weapons of Daniel's time were crude and rudimentary. One can only imagine what Daniel must have thought when he saw visions of massive tanks and armored personnel carriers thundering across the battlefield, crushing everything in their paths; jet fighters soaring through the heavens, launching fire-belching rockets, killing hundreds of people at a time; thermo-nuclear explosions that leave "*a river of fire*" in their wake, devouring entire cities. Take a look at the following images and decide for yourself if they could be interpreted in the same way as what Daniel saw.

Figure 4: *Tank Tracks that "crushed and trampled underfoot"*

Figure 5: *Soldiers on the battlefield facing "a river of fire..."*

Figure 6: *Under-wing rockets look like "large, iron teeth..."*

Figure 7: *Apache Attack Helicopter "devouring its victims"*

Now, take the proverbial keys to unleash the fire power of the world's most powerful military arsenal and hand them over to a hate-mongering lunatic like Donald Trump, and you set the stage for the most terrifying scenario in human history: Global Thermo-Nuclear War—Armageddon! Think about it. Which scenario seems more frightening: a single terrorist or rogue nation with minor nuclear capability or Donald Trump with his finger on the launch button?

A Few More Boastful Gems

"*The beauty of me is that I'm very rich.*" (ABC-TV; *Good Morning America*; March 17th, 2011) But, what have you done with all that wealth, Duck McScrooge®, to make the world a better place?

"*My Twitter® has become so powerful that I can actually make my enemies tell the truth.*" (Twitter; @realDonaldTrump; October 17th, 2012) Wow! Harry Potter® can put away his magic wand; he now can use the all-powerful *Tweeter 9000*.

"*My IQ is one of the highest – and you all know it! Please don't feel so stupid or insecure; it's not your fault.*" (Twitter; @realDonaldTrump; May 8th, 2013) No worries, Mr. T, we don't. We just feel *you're* stupid and insecure.

"*All of the women on The Apprentice flirted with me – consciously or unconsciously. That's to be expected.*" (Donald Trump; *How to Get Rich*; Random House Publishing, LLC; March 23, 2004) Perhaps they were unconscious. I mean, no self-respecting conscious woman would flirt with *that*.

"*One of the key problems today is that politics is such a disgrace. Good people don't go into government.*" (From an interview with the online magazine *The Advocate* in 2000) So…he's actually admitting he is not a good person? Well, at least he is self-aware, even if he has no filters, no scruples, no compassion, no humility, no human kindness, and no ability to relate to others.

Part One Wrap-up

The Bible constantly warns us against the negative and inciting qualities of arrogance, boasting, and the all-to-human nature to judge each other, and teaches us, instead, to humble ourselves before God. When coupled with the passages that specifically address the nature of *The Antichrist*, we can see that the future looks pretty bleak for Mr. Trump. Let's look at a few of those:

"What causes fights and quarrels among you? Don't they come from your desires that battle within you? You desire but do not have, so you kill. You covet but you cannot get what you want, so you quarrel and fight. You do not have because you do not ask God. When you ask, you do not receive, because you ask with wrong motives, that you may spend what you get on your pleasures."—James 4:1-3

"...anyone who chooses to be a friend of the world becomes an enemy of God. God opposes the proud, but shows favor to the humble."—James 4:4, 6

"As it is, you boast in your arrogant schemes. All such boasting is evil. If anyone, then, knows the good they ought to do and doesn't do it, it is sin for them."—James 4:16-17

"Do not boast about tomorrow, for you do not know what a day may bring. Let someone else praise you, and not your own mouth; an outsider, and not your own lips."—Proverbs 27:1-2

It's interesting to note, as we will examine more closely in the next section that God says he will give power to *The Antichrist* to rule for a time-period before finally destroying him.

We simply need to watch the news or listen to the

conversations around us to know that Donald Trump has indeed become a powerful presence in the current political climate. In fact, he seems to be determining and changing this country's political climate, and has made anger, accusations, name-calling and childish behavior fashionable across the entire political spectrum. Even the Democratic Candidates have recently gone on the attack, where once they maintained a calm, supportive and amiable atmosphere between themselves. Even more astonishing to me, is the large numbers of normally God-fearing, loving Christians who have embraced Mr. Trump's rhetoric of hate. As mentioned before, this is not Christian behavior. We must remember that by allowing *The Beast* to rule for a time, God is testing our faithfulness to Him. He wants to see if we have the ability to remain steadfast, following his word, and to not be swayed by the silver tongue of a politician that claims to be a believer but whose motive is purely selfish, and whose desire it is to usurp power and dominion over as many as he can. Make no mistake: Mr. Trump's intentions are anything but honorable, and we must not let ourselves become deluded by his power and influence.

"His power will be mighty, but not by his own power, and he will destroy to an extraordinary degree and prosper and perform his will; He will destroy mighty men and the holy people. And through his shrewdness He will cause deceit to succeed by his influence; and he will magnify himself in his heart, and he will destroy many while they are at ease. He will even oppose the Prince of princes[sic]…"—Daniel 8:24-25

"And it performed great signs, even causing fire to come down from heaven to the earth in full view of the people. Because of the signs it was given power to perform on behalf of the first beast, it deceived the inhabitants of the earth."—Revelation 13:13-14

Part Two:
A Rash and Deceitful King

"...watch out that no one deceives you. For many will come in my name, claiming, 'I am the Messiah,' and will deceive many. You will hear of wars and rumors of wars, but see to it that you are not alarmed. Such things must happen...Nation will rise against nation, and kingdom against kingdom. There will be famines and earthquakes in various places."

At that time many will turn away from the faith and will betray and hate each other, and many false prophets will appear and deceive many people. Because of the increase of wickedness, the love of most will grow cold..."—Matthew 24:4-7, 10-12

"*One of the heads of the beast seemed to have had a fatal wound, but the fatal wound had been healed. The whole world was filled with wonder and followed the beast.*"—Revelation 13:3

"*In the latter part of their reign, when rebels have become completely wicked, a fierce looking king, a master of intrigue, will arise.*—Daniel 8:23

A Self-Deluded Liar

The lies and deceptive maneuvering of Donald Trump are legendary. It's hard to pick an instance where he has been completely honest. Any given speech or interview may contain the seeds of truth, but it doesn't take long for Mr. Trump to bury that truth underneath lies and fabricated realities – his realities – twisted to suit his own corrupt political aspirations. Even at this writing, still two months away from the Republican National Convention, Mr. Trump insists on spewing forth his deceptive rhetoric, which makes it difficult to keep up with him. But, we will examine some his most blatant and damaging lies to date, since beginning his campaign in June of 2015. We will also look at some of his repetitive lies that he maintains as truth.

Donald Trump has been spinning tales of deceit and intrigue almost as long as he's been alive, many of which are the simple yarns of a man deluded by his wealth and his "protected" upbringing, many of which I'm sure he believes in his heart to be the truth – or at least his own twisted version of the truth. There's an old saying that if you repeat a lie enough times for long enough, not only will other people begin to believe those lies, but you yourself will begin to believe them as well. The mind is a clever machine and will re-write the lie as an accepted truth. Political maneuvering works because of this very principle. Listen to any candidate running for office, whether locally or on the federal level, and patterns will begin to emerge. You will hear certain phrases or catch words repeated over and over again, to the point where, if you listen to enough campaign speeches, the candidates start sounding like broken records. They know the value of repetition and whether it's a complete truth, a lie wrapped in a half-truth, or a blatant, outright fabrication, these "talking points" find a foothold in people's minds. The candidates' supporters, in order to sound like they know what they're talking about, then repeat these phrases and slogans when engaged in political discussions with their friends and co-workers.

To make matters worse, the media—realizing that controversial copy produces higher ratings, and higher ratings mean more revenue—have piled onto the Trump Falsehood Bandwagon, broadcasting Mr. Trump's lies to a captive and enraptured viewing public, with little to no challenge, thus perpetrating the lie, and increasing the public perception that he speaks the truth. Mr. Glenn Kessler, a fact checker for *The Washington Post*, recently made this observation:

"But the news media now faces the challenge of Donald Trump, the presumptive Republican nominee for president. Trump makes 'Four-Pinocchio' statements over and over again, even though fact checkers have demonstrated them to be false. He appears to care little about the facts; his staff does not even bother to respond to fact-checking inquiries.
But, astonishingly, television hosts rarely challenge Trump when he makes a claim that already has been found to be false. For instance, Trump says he was against the 2003 invasion of Iraq, but research by Buzzfeed found that he did express support for an attack. He said the White House even sent a delegation to tell him to tone down his statements —and we found that also to be false.
Yet at least a dozen television hosts in the past two months allowed

*Trump to make this claim and failed to challenge him. There is no excuse for th*is." (Glenn Kessler; The Washington Post Fact Check site; May7th, 2016)

Mr. Trump has given new life to the lies and myths which have circulated for years, by adopting them as the foundation of his platform. His oft-repeated assertion that people love him because he's rich and successful, demonstrates just how self-centered and deluded the man is. Political humorist and HBO talk show host John Oliver said of Donald Trump: *"I'm not even sure he knows he's lying. I think he just doesn't know what the truth is*." (John Oliver, *Last Week Tonight*, February 28, 2016). He then dispelled a plethora of self-deluding deceptions Mr. Trump enjoys repeating to his throngs of adoring fans.

Delusion One: Mr. Trump tells the truth. Through its extensive research, *Politifact*, a non-partisan fact-checking service of the *Tampa Bay Times*, found that over 75% of what Donald Trump says is "false" to one degree or another. Mr. Oliver cites many such examples to include the time the presumptive Republican nominee was invited to appear on *Last Week Tonight* five times. Mr. Oliver disputes this claim as *"completely not true.*"

Delusion Two: Mr. Trump's campaign is "self-funded". According to the *Federal Election Commission*, Donald Trump has loaned his campaign over $17 million, and gifted it an additional $250,000. This means that at the end of his campaign, he can legally pay himself back with campaign funds. Additionally, the FEC reports that Mr. Trump has taken in over $7 million from individual contributors. In my opinion, that does not constitute a "self-funded" campaign.

Delusion Three: The name Trump is synonymous with wealth and success. While it's true that Mr. Trump is a very successful real-estate mogul, and that he certainly fulfills the Biblical prophecy that *The Antichrist "...will succeed in whatever he does"*—Daniel 8:24 (NIV), he is not nearly as wealthy as he claims to be, and he has been plagued with business failures, bankruptcies, and lawsuits. These failed businesses include: *Trump Shuttle, Trump Vodka, Trump Magazine, Trump World Magazine*, the *Trump Travel* booking site *GoSite.com*, *Trump Steaks*, and *Trump Mortgage*. Many of the so called "Trump Buildings" are not even owned by Mr. Trump. He leases the license to use his name to the independent owners of those buildings.

"...a stern-faced king, a master of intrigue, will arise. He will become very strong, but not by his own power."—Daniel 8:23

I want to give particular attention to so-called *Trump University*, currently embroiled in a $40 million lawsuit initiated by New York's attorney general. The lawsuit alleges that Mr. Trump was party to a scam that promised to make students rich by teaching them Mr. Trump's secret to real estate wealth. Upwards of five-thousand students, who paid up to $35,000 to learn the secrets of getting rich in real estate, were asked to attend useless seminars that failed to deliver on the promised apprenticeships.*

"Trump University engaged in deception at every stage of

consumers' advancement through costly programs and caused real financial harm," the attorney general said. *"Trump University, with Donald Trump's knowledge and participation, relied on Trump's name recognition and celebrity status to take advantage of consumers who believed in the Trump brand."* (Eric Schneiderman; Attorney General, NY; August 23rd, 2013)

Years before, officials from the New York State Education Department found that Mr. Trump's enterprise must change its name as it did not hold an education license and that it failed to meet the legal definition of a *University*. In 2011, Mr. Trump complied, changing the name to *The Trump Entrepreneur Institute*, but has since been plagued by complaints and on-going civil lawsuits from consumers alleging it still didn't make good on its advertised claims.

"*…and it will fling truth to the ground and perform its will and prosper. … and he will magnify himself in his heart, and he will destroy many while they are at ease.*"—Daniel 8:12, 25

---

*This is a fast-developing story. As such, it is not possible to keep up with all the changes here. As of this writing, no less than three (3) class-action lawsuits—two in California and one in New York—have been brought against Mr. Trump, alleging fraud, misrepresentation, and willful deception through false advertising, among others. I will be keeping my ear to the ground regarding all aspects of these ongoing cases. Be on the lookout for a possible follow-up to this book focusing on the Trump University scandal.

The Art of the Deception

"...a king will arise, insolent and skilled in intrigue. His power will be mighty... and he will destroy to an extraordinary degree and prosper and perform his will; he will destroy mighty men and the holy people. And through his shrewdness he will cause deceit to succeed by his influence..."—Daniel 8:23-25

The most baffling aspect to Mr. Trump's outright lies and fabrications is the blind faith with which so many follow him, believing his falsehoods and accepting them as truth, simply because he has spoken it. We've already seen how the prophet Daniel foresaw that *The Antichrist* would magnify himself in the eyes of the world, so much so, that he would consider himself a god, even the savior of mankind. The unbelievable phenomenon of the throngs of loyal followers Trump has amassed around him was actually prophesied by the Apostle Paul while receiving his vision of the end of days in the Book of Revelation:

The whole world was filled with wonder and followed the beast."—Revelation 13:3

The visions and prophecies of old are coming to pass before our very eyes. These are the days of which Daniel and Paul and Matthew and Jesus and all the prophets and apostles warned us about. There is no denying it. Try as we might, there is nothing we can do to stop the prophecies from being fulfilled. We can, however, take heed and guard against being led astray by Mr. Trump's deceptions, and to remain steadfast. No matter what Mr. Trump, or any politician for that matter, tells you, there is only one

God, and no man will ever take His place.

During a December 2015 GOP Debate, Donald Trump gave what could probably be considered the worst answer ever to a debate question. Moderator Hugh Hewitt asked Mr. Trump the following question:

"What is your priority among our nuclear triad?" (Hugh Hewitt; CNN; GOP debate, December 2015)

For the benefit of those who may not know, or who may have forgotten, the *Nuclear Triad* refers to the United States' capability to deploy nuclear weapons from air, land, and sea platforms. In other words, the US has the ability to launch nuclear weapons from long-range bombers, land-based silos, and submarines. These three platforms constitute the *Nuclear Triad*. Rather than ask for clarification so he could give a reasonably intelligent answer, Mr. Trump decided to wing it, and responded:

"Well, first of all, I think we need somebody absolutely that we can trust, who is totally responsible, who really knows what he or she is doing. That is so powerful and so important. And one of the things that I'm frankly most proud of is that in 2003, 2004, I was totally against going into Iraq because you're going to destabilize the Middle East. I called it. I called it very strongly. And it was very important." (Donald Trump, GOP Presidential Debate, December 2015)

Okay, first of all, Mr. Trump has not yet answered Mr. Hewitt's question, but even worse, he lied about *"calling it"* regarding the war in Iraq. It wasn't until 2004, when the United States was already deeply embroiled for over a year in the Iraq War that Mr. Trump ever made any statements that we should not go into Iraq. (The media fact-checking service *Buzz Feed* reported that, in 2003, Donald Trump was allegedly in favor of attacking Iraq, prior to the actual invasion.) It doesn't take any great insight to make a call against an action, a year or more after that action has taken place. He didn't *call* anything! And to attempt to deceive the American people by proclaiming he foresaw the dangers of going into Iraq in the first place is exactly the kind of hypocrisy the Bible warns us against. But Mr. Trump's answer to Hugh Hewitt's question regarding the *Nuclear Triad* didn't stop there:

"But we have to be extremely vigilant and extremely careful when it comes to nuclear. Nuclear changes the whole ball game. Frankly, I would have said get out of Syria; get out—if we didn't have the power of weaponry today. The power is so massive that we can't just leave areas that fifty years ago or seventy-five years ago we wouldn't care. It was hand-to-hand combat." (Ibid.)

Are you kidding me? Seventy years ago we dropped a nuclear bomb on Japan, effectively ending World War II. Yet Mr. Trump would have us believe that even fifty years ago we were still fighting each other with swords and spears! But, he had still not answered Mr. Hewitt's question. So Mr. Trump blathered on:

"The biggest problem this world has today is not President Obama with Global Warming, which is inconceivable; this is what he's saying. The biggest problem we have is nuclear—nuclear proliferation and having some maniac, having some madman go out and get a nuclear weapon. That's in my opinion, that [sic] is

the single biggest problem that our country faces right now." (Ibid.)

Not content to leave it rest at that, Mr. Hewitt rephrased the question in hopes that Mr. Trump might more clearly understand:

"Of the three legs of the triad, though, do you have a priority? I want to go to Senator Rubio after that and ask him." (Hugh Hewitt; CNN; GOP debate, December 2015)

Mr. Trump's answer is classic Trump misdirection:

"I think—I think, for me, nuclear is just the power. The devastation is very important to me." (Donald Trump, GOP Presidential Debate, December 2015)

It is frightening that this man, with his lack of knowledge when it comes to foreign policy and the nuclear capability of the United States, wants to be the Commander-in-Chief of the most powerful nation in the free world. Even more frightening, now that Mr. Cruz and Mr. Kasich have suspended their campaigns, is that Mr. Trump is now the presumptive Republican nominee, demonstrating that many good people are falling victim to his deceptions and to his lies and to his cunning and intriguing words, and are blindly following him. This tells me that the prophecies regarding *The Antichrist* are coming to pass exactly as foretold in the Bible. And this is just the tip of the proverbial iceberg.

America is Already Great!

Perhaps the most insidious, and therefore most damaging, lie Mr. Trump proliferates is the implication that America has somehow fallen from grace and is no longer the greatest nation on the face of the planet.

The greatness of a country is not measured in brick and mortar. It's not measured by its soaring skyscrapers, or by the expanse of its newest sports complex. The greatness of a country should not be measured by the strength of its economy, or by the income levels of its consumers. The greatness of a country is not measured by who owns the most real estate, or by who owns the latest and most expensive "toys". The greatness of a country should not even be measured by the growth percentage of its Gross Domestic Product, or by its fluctuating unemployment rate. Skyscrapers, sports centers, cars, houses, and all material possessions are temporary; eventually they succumb to the forces of nature and to entropy, and crumble to dust. Economic growth, the GDP, the unemployment rate, and all such metrics fluctuate on a regular basis, rising and falling with the global markets, like waves on an open ocean. Some years are fat and some years are lean. While these are important factors in the economic strength of a nation, they should not serve as the measuring sticks of a country's *greatness*.

My friends; the greatness of a country is measured in its people—*in you and me*—and in how we treat each other as human beings and as members of the family of humankind. And although we too are temporary, and will all one day succumb to the forces of entropy, and return to the dust of the Earth, *we, the people*, are what make America great.

It's the people who built the skyscrapers and the sports arenas; it's the people who built the factories to manufacture the cars we drive and the products we consume; it's the people who toiled under the blazing sun to till the land and grow the crops that feed a nation; it's the people who built the railroads, the trucks, the aircraft, and the ships that transport those goods across this great land, and around the world. From the first colonists who landed on our eastern shores, to the explorers and the pioneers who struck out across the Great Plains, forded the mighty rivers, and scaled the majestic Rocky Mountains, enduring sickness and death, not stopping until they reached shining waters of the Pacific Ocean, it's the people who blazed the trails and paved the roads and highways so that others could follow.

It's the people who work the midnight hours as our first responders: the firemen who enter burning buildings while the rest of us run out; the police officers who patrol the killing fields and drug lanes of our inner cities, maintaining the thin blue line of protection, bringing to justice the criminal elements while we sleep safe in our warm beds; the doctors, nurses, and paramedics who work tirelessly in hospitals and accident scenes across this great land, to ensure another heart keeps beating.

It's the people who volunteer to serve as Soldiers, Sailors, Marines, Airmen, and Coast Guardsmen—members of the most powerful military machine on Earth—rushing into harm's way with no forethought of their own safety, knowing they must "hold the line" at all costs, willing to make the ultimate sacrifice so the rest of us can live with the freedoms we enjoy, and so often take for granted.

It's the people who made—and still do make—America great!

Mr. Trump and his followers need only to open their eyes to see that every day in this great country of ours people quietly and anonymously perform random acts of kindness for their fellow Americans. They don't do it for recognition, or fame, or money, or accolades, but simply out of the goodness of their own hearts; because it's the right thing to do. They selflessly follow the Golden Rule:

"So, in everything, do to others what you would have them do to you."—Matthew 7:12

Hurrying through a crowded subway station to avoid missing his train, a young man sees an elderly woman struggling down the station steps, laden with heavy grocery bags. He stops to help her down the stairs and over to her platform. He misses his train, but gains something far greater in return.

A middle-class suburban woman, standing in line at the supermarket check-out counter notices a young, impoverished single mother unable to pay for her food because she doesn't have enough money. Without hesitation, the woman pays for the young mother's groceries.

A wealthy businessman stops by his local Wal-Mart™ store and anonymously pays off all of the Christmas lay-a-way accounts; a total of $20,000.

A Marine, leading his squad of infantrymen through the malaria-infested swamps of the Vietnamese jungle, watches as an enemy hand grenade drops a few feet in front of him. Though tired, hungry, and homesick, he immediately reacts, throwing himself on top of the grenade, allowing his body to absorb the brunt of the explosion; sacrificing himself so his squad members can live.

These are the things that make America great! And it happens every day, in large cities and small towns all across this great land. We see it in the smiles of the people we pass on the street. We hear it in the laughter of young and old alike. We feel it in our own hearts, when we reach out to someone in need, not expecting anything in return.

"Cast thy bread upon the waters; for thou shalt find it after many days. Give a portion to seven, yea, even unto eight; for thou knowest not what evil shall be upon the earth...He that observeth the wind shall not sow; and he that regardeth the clouds shall not reap...In the morning sow thy seed, and in the evening withhold not thy hand; for thou knowest not which shall prosper, whether this or that, or whether they both shall be alike good."— Ecclesiastes 11:1-2, 4, 6

So, when Donald Trump implies that America is no longer great, but that he, and he alone, has the solutions to making "*America great again*", you have to ask yourself: is he that insecure and delusional that he has lost faith in you, the very people who have made this country the greatest country on the planet? Is he that arrogant and narcissistic that he believes he can somehow wave his *Magic Trump Wand* and immediately solve all of our problems? Or is it all a well-crafted, meticulously planned lie; a ruse; a deception, carefully designed and calculated to pull the proverbial wool over your eyes, to blind you from the truth that America *is* great, and it doesn't need fixing?

These are the tactics of a dictator: to paint a bleak picture of the current state of the union, and then, once he has hooked you into believing that lie, to cast himself in the role of the redeemer, proclaiming and promising to unify the country while secretly plotting to usurp absolute power over everyone and everything. You do it his way or you're out! Don't believe me, go back and revisit the hateful rhetoric he has spewed out at debates and rallies. Go back and read his misogynistic and boastful tweets.

Have you heard the story about how to successfully cook a frog?

If you take the frog and toss him into a pot of boiling water, he will immediately sense danger and will jump out. However, if you place him gently in a pot of cool water, then gradually turn up the heat, bit by bit, letting the frog get comfortable and complacent, by the time the danger becomes evident, it will be too late. The frog will no longer have the strength or the will to jump out of the pot and will slowly cook to death. That is what Mr. Trump is doing to his followers, and it's what he will do to the country if elected President. He is not your friend, he is not a unifier, and he is most certainly not a believer.

I know we do not live in a utopian society, and I'm not so naïve to think that we do. Of course there is crime. Of course people struggle just to make ends meet. Of course we have homelessness and inner-city blight. Of course the cost of consumer goods continues to rise and the value of education continues to decline. This country has its share of challenges and problems. But, my dear friends, that does not mean America is not great!

America is one giant family, more than 300 million strong, comprised of the ethnic diversity of immigrants who came here from every continent around the world, seeking a better life for themselves and for their loved ones. And, just like with any family, our great American family has its share of challenges and problems to overcome. But, just because your family may experience financial challenges from time to time; just because your family may struggle with a wayward son or daughter who runs into trouble with the law; just because your family may experience strife and disagreement and arguments; just because your family faces problems, doesn't mean you throw up your hands and declare that your family is no longer great. In your eyes, your family will always be great, and you will always love them, no matter what. Why? Because they belong to you!

The economy, universal health care, wage and tax equality, immigration reform, and the myriad other laws and acts that come out of Washington, D.C., are all works-in-progress. We too are a work-in-progress. No one is perfect, and for Mr. Trump to imply that, just because he thinks he's been somehow divinely appointed to fix America's problems, and that America won't be "great again" until he does so, is pure hubris. It demonstrates just how cunning and deceitful his intentions really are.

A House Built Upon the Sand

We all know what happens to a building if you remove its foundation: it crumbles to the ground. The Bible warns us against building our lives on unstable foundations:

"Everyone who hears these words of mine and does not act on them, will be like a foolish man who built his house on the sand. The rain fell, and the floods came, and the winds blew and slammed against that house; and it fell-- and great was its fall."— Matthew 7:26-27

The falsehood that America is not great is at the heart of Donald Trump's campaign slogan to *"Make America Great Again"*, and has become the foundation upon which his entire campaign of hate and rhetoric has been built. But that foundation is nothing but shifting sand and cannot endure the test of time.

We've already determined where America's true greatness lies, but let's take a moment and look at the issue from Mr. Trump's point-of-view to see why his rhetoric is nothing but smoke and mirrors—a house built on shifting sands. Judging from some of Mr. Trump's key talking points on the campaign trail, we can infer that *his* definition of an America that's *great* is one in which jobs are on the increase, the Affordable Care Act (Obamacare) is repealed, and the budget deficit is brought down. (I know he prattles on about many other issues such as global terrorism, 2nd Amendment Rights, Pro-choice v. Pro-life, and the current strength of the US military—all important issues to be sure—but let's just look at the above three). His now famous line from his June 2015 candidacy announcement speech set the tone for his entire campaign of lies, cunning, and deception:

"*I will be the greatest jobs president that God has ever created.*" (Donald Trump; June 16th, 2015; from his Presidential Campaign announcement speech at Trump Tower)

Okay. So what's the truth behind the rhetoric?

Mr. Trump claims that America will be great again if we appeal Obamacare, because he believes it to be a job killer and denies its effectiveness as a viable health care option. Well, let's look at that.

In a 2015 study, the Bureau of Labor Statistics determined that between the first quarter of 2010, when the Affordable Care Act was passed, and the third quarter of 2014, *9.8 million private-sector jobs* were created. This is in addition to the steady jobs increase which began shortly after President Obama took office and signed the *American Recovery and Reinvestment Act of 2009*, also known as *The Stimulus*. **(See Appendix: figures 8 and 9)**

And what about the claim that Obamacare is not working?

In their 2015 National Health Interview Survey, the Centers for Disease Control (CDC) and the National Center for Health Statistics (NCHS) reported a sharp and steady decline in the share of uninsured Americans—10.7 percent, the lowest going all the way back to 1972—since the Affordable Care Act was signed into law. To further illustrate that Obamacare is in fact working, a grass roots organization known as *The Other 98%* delineated ten benefits of the Affordable Care Act; benefits that Mr. Trump plans to take away from you by repealing Obamacare. They include access to affordable health insurance for 30 million Americans previously uninsured, mandatory insurance coverage for those with pre-existing conditions, and discounts for seniors on brand-name prescription medication, plus many more. **(See Appendix: figures 10 and 11)**

What about the unemployment rate as a factor that makes America great?

Mr. Trump would have you believe that nearly 50% of all Americans are currently unemployed. This is a gross exaggeration which we will visit in more detail later in this section. For now, let's just look at the big picture. We've already seen how the ACA added over nine million new jobs to the private sector. It naturally follows that there should be a decline in the unemployment rate. Again, since Mr. Obama took office, the unemployment rate has been on a steady decline, compared with the sharp increase in the final year of the George W. Bush Administration. **(See Appendix: figures 12 and 13)**

Lastly, let's look at the budget deficit, which Mr. Trump claims is the highest in history, thus implying that America is no longer great. What about that?

In April, 2014, the Congressional Budget Office—a federal agency within the legislative branch of the United States government that provides budget and economic information to Congress—showed that in the five year period between when President Obama took office and when the report was filed, the budget deficit fell sharply from 9.8% in Fiscal Year 2009 to 2.8%

in FY 2014. The CBO linked this decline, just as with job growth, to the passing of the Affordable Care Act in 2010. **(See Appendix: figures 14 and 15)**

Ergo, by Mr. Trump's own criteria for measuring the greatness of a nation, *America is already great!*

By implying that America is not already great and that he can miraculously make it so, Mr. Trump is treading on dangerous ground. He's building his house on a foundation that has no chance of standing firm against the proverbial storms that will rage against him.

A Fatal Wound is Healed

Let's look again at what the apostle Paul tells us in Revelation about *The Antichrist*:

"One of the heads of the beast seemed to have had a fatal wound, but the fatal wound had been healed. The whole world was filled with wonder and followed the beast."—Revelation 13:3

In the April 2016 Primaries, Donald Trump faltered, as he lost the states of Colorado and Wyoming to his political rivals. His Republican colleagues banded against him; threatening to hold a contested Republican Convention should he gain the most delegates, but not the nomination. He was getting hammered from all sides and still stubbornly refused to set his ship right. This could be classified as the fatal wound of which Paul spoke, which wound was later healed. Even after his setbacks in Wyoming and Colorado, Mr. Trump was still the Republican front-runner. Then, on May 3rd, Donald Trump won the Indiana Republican Primaries by a landslide, prompting both Senator Ted Cruz, and Governor John Kasich to suspend their respective campaigns. This left Mr. Trump as the sole contender for the Republican nomination and as the presumptive nominee for the Republican Party. The "fatal" wound had been healed. Paul's prophetic vision had been fulfilled. It could be argued that the class-action lawsuits against Mr. Trump and the Trump University fiasco, and the incredible backlash— even from his own party members—from Mr. Trump's alleged racist remarks regarding Judge Curiel's Mexican heritage, could also be considered "fatal" wounds to Trump's political aspirations.

The outcome, and whether or not he heals from those wounds, is yet to be seen.

Deceiving the American People

"And on account of transgression the host will be given over to the horn along with the regular sacrifice; and it will fling truth to the ground and perform its will and prosper."—Daniel 8:12

"When the transgressors have run their course, a king will arise, insolent and skilled in intrigue. His power will be mighty, but not by his own power, and he will destroy to an extraordinary degree and prosper and perform his will; he will destroy mighty men and the holy people. And through his shrewdness he will cause deceit to succeed by his influence; and he will magnify himself in his heart, and he will destroy many while they are at ease. He will even oppose the Prince of princes, but he will be broken without human agency. The vision of the evenings and mornings which has been told is true; but keep the vision secret, for it pertains to many days in the future."—Daniel 8:22-26

We have already pointed out that the Prophets and Apostles of Biblical times prophesied that many would be deceived by the cunning and intrigue of *The Antichrist*, so much so that they would believe his lies and follow him. Just look how many people defend the completely unconstitutional and, dare I say it, un-American, rhetoric that Mr. Trump spews forth every time he opens his mouth. He has mastered the art of deception. He has perfected the science of making lies appear as the truth through careful manipulation of words and by convincing his listeners and followers that what he says is what they want to hear. It's the same tactics he has used for decades in his real estate dealings, and why he has become so successful…in the secular world; but certainly not in a spiritual sense.

As mentioned in the introduction to this book, he himself espouses to the words of the late P.T. Barnum that *"there's a sucker born every minute"*, and uses that *sucker principle* to his advantage and for personal gain. Do not think for a minute that Mr. Trump has the best interests at heart for the American People. Far from it. The only person Donald Trump truly cares about is Donald Trump. Don't believe me? Listen carefully to him when he speaks. It's always about himself, usually at the expense of others, to include members of his own party. These are not the words of a man who has America's values and best interests at heart. These are also not the words of a man of confidence and compassion. On the contrary; Mr. Trump seems to me to be very insecure, and he hides his insecurities behind his lies and narcissistic boasting. He comes across as nothing but a sad, pathetic little five-year-old—a spoiled child—who throws his *Trumper-tantrums* whenever he doesn't get his way. He then takes that anger and turns it into cunning deception, just as the Bible has told us *The Antichrist* would do.

In January 2016, Mr. Trump chose to boycott the GOP Presidential Debate in Iowa because he allegedly felt he was being treated unfairly by Fox News Journalist and debate moderator Megyn Kelly, choosing instead to hold a rally at a nearby venue, ostensibly as a fund raiser for Veterans' Organizations to support America's wounded warriors.

As a veteran of Operation Iraqi Freedom myself, and as a sufferer of PTSD and TBI, I was surprised to hear that the usual bombastic, self-centered, boastful, cunning and deceitful Mr.

Trump might actually be doing something noble. My surprise was short-lived. The over six million dollars that Mr. Trump ostensibly raised were funneled into his own organization, *The Donald J. Trump Foundation*, through which the funds were then supposed to be dispersed out to various Veterans groups. The Foundation even produced a list of 22 Veterans Charities amongst whom the funds were to be divided. Notably, two major Veterans' Organizations were not included on Trump's List, *the Iraq and Afghanistan Veterans of America* and *VoteVets*, both of which had recently called Trump out for using veterans to distract American voters from his debate problems.

What was it that Daniel said about *The Antichrist*'s cunning and intrigue?

It's interesting to note that, since 2010, the *Trump Foundation* has donated less than $75,000 to Veterans' Groups. Not the philanthropic actions of a billionaire who claims to love and support America's Veterans.

Jon Soltz of *votevets.org*, one of the Veterans' Groups intentionally left off of the *Trump Beneficiary List*, talks about Donald Trump's decision not to attend the Fox GOP debate and to hold a veterans event instead saying, "*...there's absolutely no substance behind him when it comes to helping veterans.*" (See the entire four-and-a-half minute interview by clicking on the VoteVets link above.)

The Wall Street Journal, in an effort to find out what happened to the over six million dollars raised by Mr. Trump, contacted 19 of the 22 Veterans' Charities on the *Trump Foundation* list. They could only account for approximately $2.4 million. That still leaves over $4 million unaccounted for. Did Mr. Trump pocket the money himself? Did he use it to help continue to fund his Presidential Campaign? No one knows as there is no clear accountability as to what happened to the money. This much is certain: Mr. Trump lied unabashedly about his desire to help the wounded American Veterans who have sacrificed so much for this *great* country of ours! This offends me, as it should offend any red-blooded American who prefers compassion over greed and corruption.*

"And through his shrewdness he will cause deceit to succeed by his influence; and he will magnify himself in his heart, and he will destroy many while they are at ease."—Daniel 8:25

And so we continue to see Daniel's prophecies fulfilled almost to the letter. There is little doubt in my mind and in my heart that Daniel was indeed seeing these, the end of days and in particular, the rise and eventual downfall of Mr. Donald Trump.

The vision of the evenings and mornings which has been told is true; but keep the vision secret, for it pertains to many days in the future."—Daniel 8:26

---

*Responding to the relentless hounding by the media he has received since his claim in January that he had raised over $6 million for Veterans' Organizations, Mr. Trump called a press conference on Tuesday, May 31st to ostensibly account for the money. *The Daily Beast* reported that, of the twenty veterans' charities they had reached out to, fifteen responded, all of them saying they had received the funds Mr. Trump claims to have sent them. However, most of the checks were allegedly dated May 24 or later, making me wonder just how much interest Mr. Trump received while the millions he raised in January rested quietly in a high-yield, interest-bearing account.

Liar, Liar, Pants on Fire

PolitiFact, a non-partisan fact-checking website run by the *Tampa Bay Times*, conducts extensive research on the claims politicians and business leaders make, and then, based on their fact-finding research, rates the claims on their *Truth-O-Meter®*. The scale ranges from *"True"* on the one end of the spectrum, all the way to *"Pants-on-fire"* at the other end. As noted earlier, *PolitiFact* has concluded that over 75% of Donald Trump's claims range from *"Mostly False"* all the way to *"Pants-on-fire"*. Many fall into the last category.

What follows are some of the most outlandish claims Mr. Trump has made and *PolitiFact's* response and ruling.

Mr. Trump's entire political platform is based on the premise that he (and he alone) will *"make America great again"*, continuing to perpetrate the covert deception that America is somehow not already great! One of Mr. Trump's many, and oft repeated, talking points is that America is not great because the economy is ostensibly in shambles. Even though we've already addressed this over-arching deception, I thought it would be interesting to get *PolitiFact's* take.

For decades, two of the indicators of the strength of our economy have been the unemployment percentage rate, and the growth in the GDP (Gross Domestic Product) over consecutive quarters. I'm not an economist, I'm a writer, but even I can see the flaws in Mr. Trump's interpretations of these two economic barometers. Let's look at what Trump said, and how *PolitiFact* discredited his claims.

The Deception: "*Don't believe those phony numbers when you hear 4.9 and 5 percent unemployment. The number's probably 28, 29, as high as 35. In fact, I even heard recently 42 percent.*" (Donald Trump, February 9th, 2016, New Hampshire primary victory speech)

PolitiFact Response: "*Actually, Trump's the one who shouldn't be believed. Numbers that high are not even close to accurate. During January 2016 the unemployment rate was 4.9 percent, its lowest level since February 2008. Not factored into this calculation, however, are people not currently looking for work.*" (PolitiFact, February 11th, 2016; Louis Jacobson, Angie Drobnic Holan, and Amy Hollyfield)

According to *PolitiFact's* findings, we can include in the category of Americans currently not looking for work the 39.2 million people ages 16-19, and those age 65 and older, who are not currently in the work force; the 13 million full-time college students; the 10.4 million stay-at-home moms; the two-million stay-at-home dads; and the almost 9 million Americans currently receiving disability compensation. This leaves an estimated 10.5 million who could legitimately be considered *unemployed*, or to put it another way, 15.6 percent. That's certainly higher than the official rates, but still a far cry from Mr. Trump's outlandish figure of 42 percent.

By failing to consider the above calculations in his claims of the "real" unemployment rate, Mr. Trump artfully deceives Americans into believing that this country is not "great", but that we should not be afraid, because he will save us!

PolitiFact's final ruling: *While economists say that there are other, more expansive calculations…none of the official ones are* *currently higher than 9.9 percent, and the highest credible number we could calculate was 15.6 percent. That's far, far lower than 42 percent -- or even 28 percent. We rate the claim* **Pants on Fire** (ibid.)

At that time many will turn away from the faith and will betray and hate each other, and many false prophets will appear and deceive many people. Because of the increase of wickedness, the love of most will grow cold…"—Matthew 24:10-12

The Deception: "*GDP was zero essentially for the last two quarters. We're at zero, we're not doing anything.*" (Donald Trump, March 10th, 2016; Miami GOP debate)

Again, Mr. Trump is using the widely held misconception that our economy's growth is dead, to support his claim that America isn't "great" anymore. As a successful businessman, Mr. Trump should know that his numbers are false, but he spins them to his benefit, thereby continuing to deceive the American people, and lead *"even the very elect"* away from the truth.

PolitiFact Response: *Assuming that Trump was talking about growth in GDP and not the real gross domestic product, his statement that it's zero is an exaggeration. In reality, GDP grew at an annual rate of 1 percent in the fourth quarter of 2015, and 2 percent in the third quarter*, according to the Bureau of Economic Analysis.
PolitiFact's final ruling: *Trump said, "GDP was zero essentially for the last two quarters". Economic growth in the last two quarters of 2015 was modest: 1 percent and 2 percent. But that's not zero. We rate Trump's claim False.* (PolitiFact; March 11th, 2016; Louis Jacobson, Linda Qiu, and Katie Sanders)

To further underscore Mr. Trump's unapologetic deceptions regarding the United States' economic growth, during his June 2015 presidential announcement speech he tried to make the claim that the growth in the GDP had dropped below zero the previous quarter; an all-time low. He said:

"*The last quarter, it was just announced, our gross domestic product—a sign of strength, right? But not for us. It was below zero. Who ever heard of this? It's never below zero.*" (Donald Trump; June 16th, 2015; Presidential Announcement Speech)

PolitiFact gave that claim a *Pants on Fire* rating as well, pointing out that GDP growth had dropped below zero at least 42 times since 1914, including five times during the George W. Bush administration: twice in 2001, and three times in 2008. (PolitiFact; June 16th 2015)

So, again, Mr. Trump's claim that the negative growth in the GDP during the first quarter of 2015—it fell by 0.7 percent—was the only time in recorded history the GDP has experienced negative growth is just another one of his many scare tactics to try to deceive the American people and to cast himself in the role of America's redeemer. Just to clarify, a negative growth pattern in the GDP from quarter to quarter is one of the indicators of a recession; of which there have been eleven since World War Two.

Let's look at another blatant lie Mr. Trump likes repeating, not because he believes what he's saying, but rather because he knows his lies appeal to the Republican base. As mentioned before, it's a tactic he uses, learned from his years of negotiating multi-million dollar business deals, to gather followers around him. Do I really need to quote the Prophet Daniel again?

On Sunday, January 10th, 2016 on NBC's Meet the Press, Mr. Trump repeated the oft heard and oft believed misconception that President Obama's decision to exchange five Guantanamo Bay detainees for Taliban prisoner US Army Sergeant Bowe Bergdahl in May of 2014 was one of the worst deals the President ever negotiated.

The Deception: "*I always bring up Bergdahl,*" Mr. Trump said in the interview. "*We get a traitor, they get five people that they've wanted for nine years, and they're back on the battlefield, trying to kill everybody, including us. And we get a dirty, rotten traitor.*" (Donald Trump, Meet the Press, January 10th, 2016; Ottumwa, Iowa)

Though certainly not a popular decision, this action was not the first time the US has exchanged prisoners with our enemies. According to military historians, prisoner exchanges have been standard practice for the United States in times of war, dating all the way back to the Revolutionary War, a fact that Mr. Trump artfully ignores. In fact, George W. Bush, known for his oft repeated mantra that the U.S. does not negotiate with terrorists, engaged in numerous negotiations with terrorist organizations.

Under President George W. Bush, Charles "Cully" Stimson, a security expert at the conservative Heritage Foundation think tank, helped coordinate the Pentagon's detainee operations in Iraq, Afghanistan, Guantanamo Bay, Cuba, and other places around the world. He said presidential administrations of both political parties routinely have been forced to deal with terrorist groups for "information, supplies, personnel [sic] -- a lot of different topics." (Media Matters for America; June 3rd, 2014)

"We have had very quiet negotiations or discussions at least, with terrorist groups over the years on a whole host of things," Stimson went on to say. *"They just haven't usually come to light."* (ibid.)

Mr. Trump's assertion that the prisoners President Obama released—all senior Taliban operatives—are *"back on the battlefield"* is based not in fact, but rather on faulty intelligence, and was discredited as *"false"* by PolitiFact's crack research team:

PolitiFact Response: *The Taliban Five...they're still where they were last -- in the Persian Gulf nation of Qatar under government supervision.*
The five detainees were released to Qatar in 2014. Qatar is understood to be a neutral state, as opposed to a "battlefield" for insurgent activity. Under the agreement, the five released detainees are not allowed to leave the country.
In December 2015, the Republican-controlled House Armed Services Committee...noted that the security arrangements first made in 2015 had been extended so that the five would remain in Qatar.
PolitiFact's final ruling: *Because there is no evidence to support Trump's claim, we rate it False.* (PolitiFact; January 10th, 2016; Lauren Carroll and Angie Drobnic Holan)

I think that's enough. If you're interested in reading more about the lies and deceptions on which PolitiFact's research team has called out Mr. Trump, just visit their website at PolitiFact.com.

(Just in case anyone is wondering, I do not receive any commissions from any of the endorsements I make in this book.

They are merely part of the extensive research and fact-checking that went into this work.)

It's fair to say that just about anything that comes out of Mr. Donald Trump's mouth is, to a certain extent, a falsehood. Never, in all my years of federal service, have I seen a candidate for President lie as unabashedly or as often as does Mr. Trump. My guess is that he knows that most of what he says is untrue, but he also knows the power and influence of the media, and that audiences thrive on "real-life" drama and on controversial sound bites. Through his years as a real-estate mogul and reality TV star, Mr. Trump has learned how to manipulate that media, thereby manipulating his audience, to make his lies appear as truth.

"They exchanged the truth... for a lie, and worshiped and served created things rather than the Creator..."—Romans 1:25

After all, isn't *The Art of the Deal* really the art of deception, manipulation, and even the lie? During any negotiation, isn't it the one who can misdirect and out-deceive his opponent, if you will, the one who wins the negotiation? Mr. Trump literally wrote the book on the art of the deal, so it stands to reason he would use his own principles of cunning and intrigue to attempt to worm his way into the hearts and minds of American voters.

And So, At Parting

As I prepare to climb down from my soap box and bring this book to a close, I wish to leave you with a few parting thoughts.

First of all, this book is not, in any way, intended to tell you who you should or shouldn't vote for in the upcoming General Election, but instead is a plea to believers everywhere to open your eyes and to see the prophecies of old manifesting themselves to complete fulfillment in our time.

Secondly, if you have been entranced by the beguiling, silver tongue of Candidate Trump, and have decided to support his campaign for the White House, that is your choice. One of the greatest gifts that God has given us is the freedom to choose how we wish to lead our lives, but every choice has an unequivocal and certain consequence attached to it. You cannot make any choice in life without experiencing its outcome.

"Be not deceived; God is not mocked: for whatsoever a man soweth, that shall he also reap."—Galatians 6:7

But I ask you to take a step back for a moment, take a deep breath, and prayerfully ask yourself if Mr. Trump's platform and political agenda really fall in line with your own personal beliefs. If so, then by all means, more power to you. But if not, if there is even the slightest doubt that Mr. Trump has your best interests at heart; if you come to realize that he may be leading you down the proverbial primrose pathway to misery, then I urge you to reconsider.

I know that much of the content of this book has focused on

the dark and negative realities facing America under a potential Trump Presidency, so let's lighten things up a bit. In a recent Public Policy Poll, conducted May 6th through May 9th, 2016, registered voters were asked of which of the following they had a higher opinion, when compared with Donald Trump:

1) Head lice
2) Traffic jams
3) Used car salesmen
4) Hipsters
5) The Department of Motor Vehicles
6) Jury duty
7) The band *Nickleback*
8) Root canals

Even though it seems like it may be a joke, it is not. The results of the poll are real and 100 percent accurate. This poll actually took place. And though it was not intended to be a joke, but to make a sober and frightening point, the results are funny, none the less. **(See Appendix: Figure 16)**

So, is Donald Trump *The Antichrist*? I don't know. But, I do know that the evidence is certainly compelling, and that every day he himself makes that reality so much more obvious by the bombastic, narcissistic, and misogynistic things he says and does. Whether he realizes it or not, Mr. Trump has, in point of fact, taken on that proverbial mantle by exhibiting the characteristics and attitudes of *The Antichrist*, almost verbatim, as prophesied in Holy Scripture.

But, don't take my word for it. Do your own Bible Study;

research the visions of the Prophet Daniel, the Apostle Paul, and the many prophets and seers who were shown that *The Antichrist* would rise in our day and age, in explicit detail, and who warned us not to be led astray, not to fall victim to the rants and ravings of false prophets. Then look around you, not with an eye towards cynicism or judgment, but with a heart that seeks to know the truth, and ask yourself if those prophecies are not, in fact, coming true on an almost daily basis.

"Watch out for false prophets. They come to you in sheep's clothing, but inwardly they are ferocious wolves. By their fruit you will recognize them. Do people pick grapes from thornbushes, or figs from thistles? Likewise, every good tree bears good fruit, but a bad tree bears bad fruit. A good tree cannot bear bad fruit, and a bad tree cannot bear good fruit. Every tree that does not bear good fruit is cut down and thrown into the fire. Thus, by their fruit you will recognize them."—Matthew 7:15-20

And finally, I want to thank you for purchasing and reading this labor of love. It is my sincere hope that it has given you something to consider and to prayerfully think about. Whether my words have made you angry or giddy, I hope that this book will at least give you the tools and the resources you need to get the conversation going with regards to the dark and sinister agenda of *The Antichrist*, whom ever you perceive him to be.

"Ask and it will be given to you; seek and you will find; knock and the door will be opened to you. For everyone who asks receives; the one who seeks finds; and to the one who knocks, the door will be opened."—Matthew 7:7-8

If you feel so compelled, then I ask you to please leave your feedback about this book at Amazon.com. I'm sincerely interested in knowing your thoughts on my interpretation of Biblical prophecy. Your honest review will also help me in future updates to this book, or in new books that I will soon be writing.

Thank you for your time, and may God bless you, always.

Lawrence R. Moelhauser
June, 2016

Appendix
Supporting Graphs and Charts

Coverage of GOP Candidates
CNN Prime Time Weekday Shows, 8/24/2015 - 9/4/2015

1.	Donald Trump	580 minutes	77.57%
2.	Jeb Bush	88 minutes	11.75%
3.	Ben Carson	41 minutes	5.50%
4.	Scott Walker	10 minutes	1.29%
5.	Carly Fiorina	8 minutes	1.11%
6.	Marco Rubio	6 minutes	0.80%
7.	Jim Gilmore	6 minutes	0.76%
8.	Ted Cruz	3 minutes	0.35%
9.	Rick Perry	2 minutes	0.32%
10.	Chris Christie	2 minutes	0.23%
11.	Lindsey Graham	2 minutes	0.20%
12.	Rand Paul	2 minutes	0.07%
13.	Bobby Jindal	9 seconds	0.02%
14.	John Kasich	6 seconds	0.01%
15.	Mike Huckabee	6 seconds	0.01%
16.	Rick Santorum	6 seconds	0.01%
17.	George Pataki	– zero –	0.00%

Source: Media Research Center

Figure 3: Television Coverage of GOP Candidates

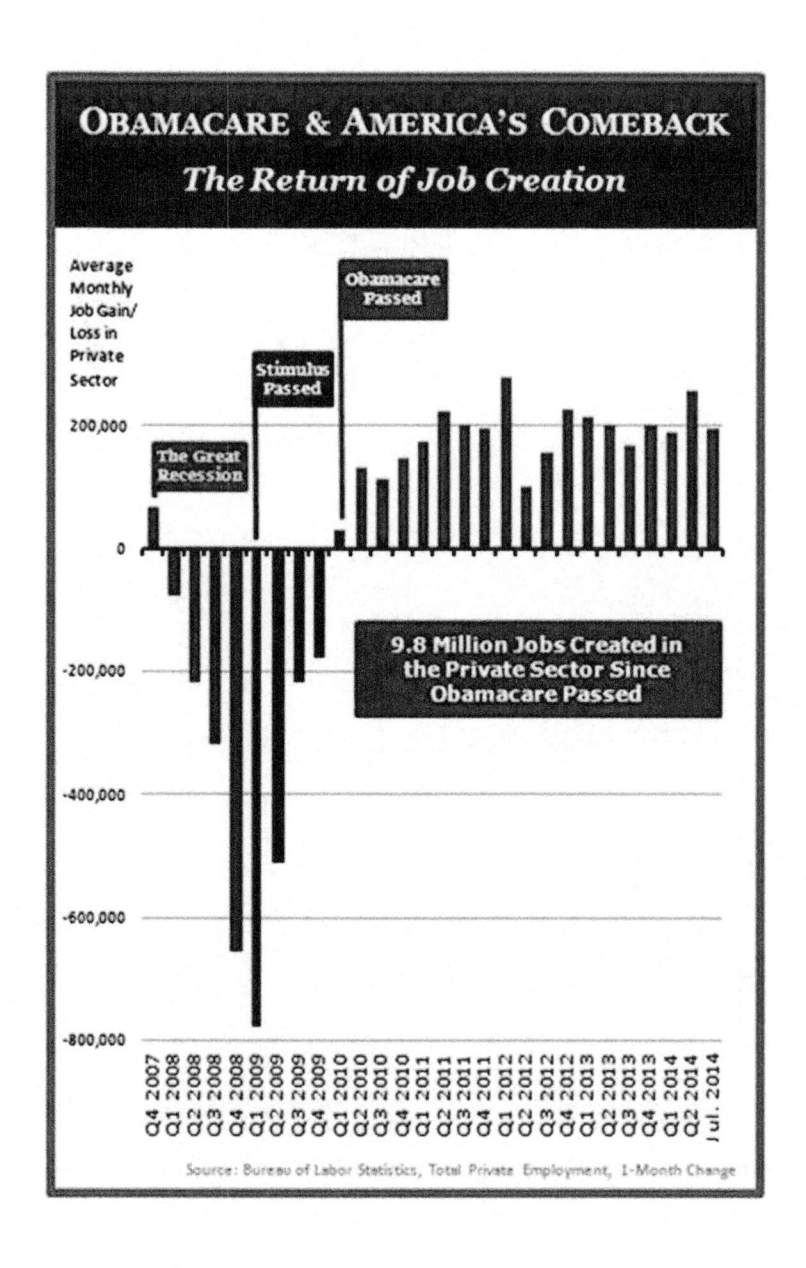

Figure 8: The Return of Job Creation since Obamacare

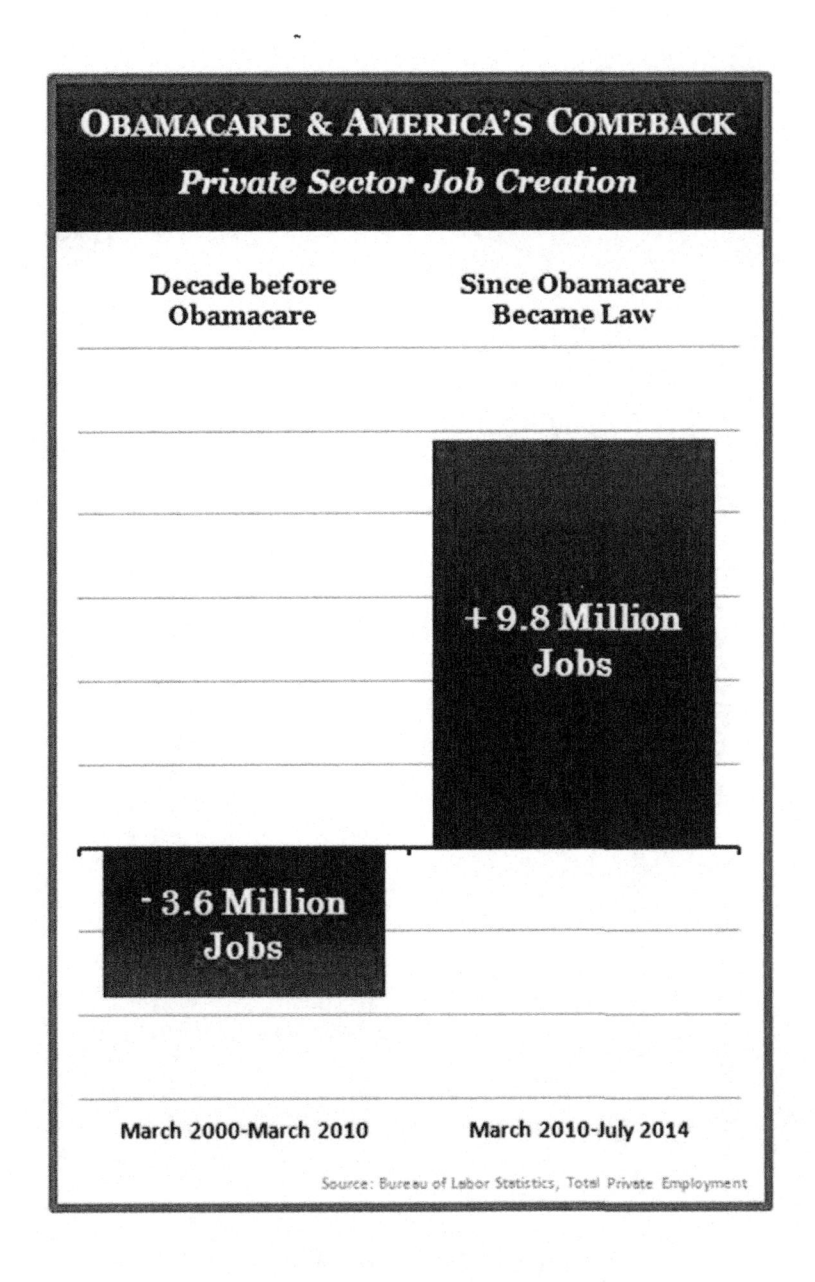

Figure 9: Private Sector Job Creation since Obamacare

Figure 10: Uninsured Rate Decline since ObamaCare

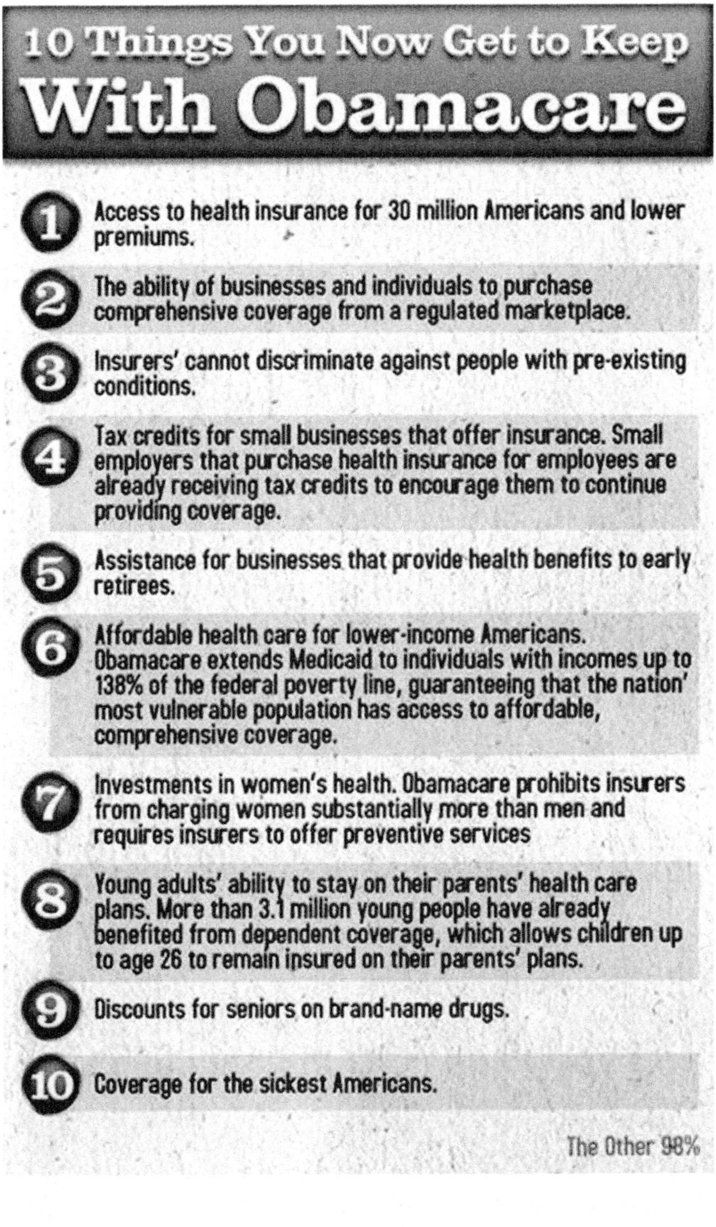

10 Things You Now Get to Keep With Obamacare

1. Access to health insurance for 30 million Americans and lower premiums.

2. The ability of businesses and individuals to purchase comprehensive coverage from a regulated marketplace.

3. Insurers' cannot discriminate against people with pre-existing conditions.

4. Tax credits for small businesses that offer insurance. Small employers that purchase health insurance for employees are already receiving tax credits to encourage them to continue providing coverage.

5. Assistance for businesses that provide health benefits to early retirees.

6. Affordable health care for lower-income Americans. Obamacare extends Medicaid to individuals with incomes up to 138% of the federal poverty line, guaranteeing that the nation' most vulnerable population has access to affordable, comprehensive coverage.

7. Investments in women's health. Obamacare prohibits insurers from charging women substantially more than men and requires insurers to offer preventive services

8. Young adults' ability to stay on their parents' health care plans. More than 3.1 million young people have already benefited from dependent coverage, which allows children up to age 26 to remain insured on their parents' plans.

9. Discounts for seniors on brand-name drugs.

10. Coverage for the sickest Americans.

The Other 98%

Figure 11: Ten Things You Get to Keep with Obamacare

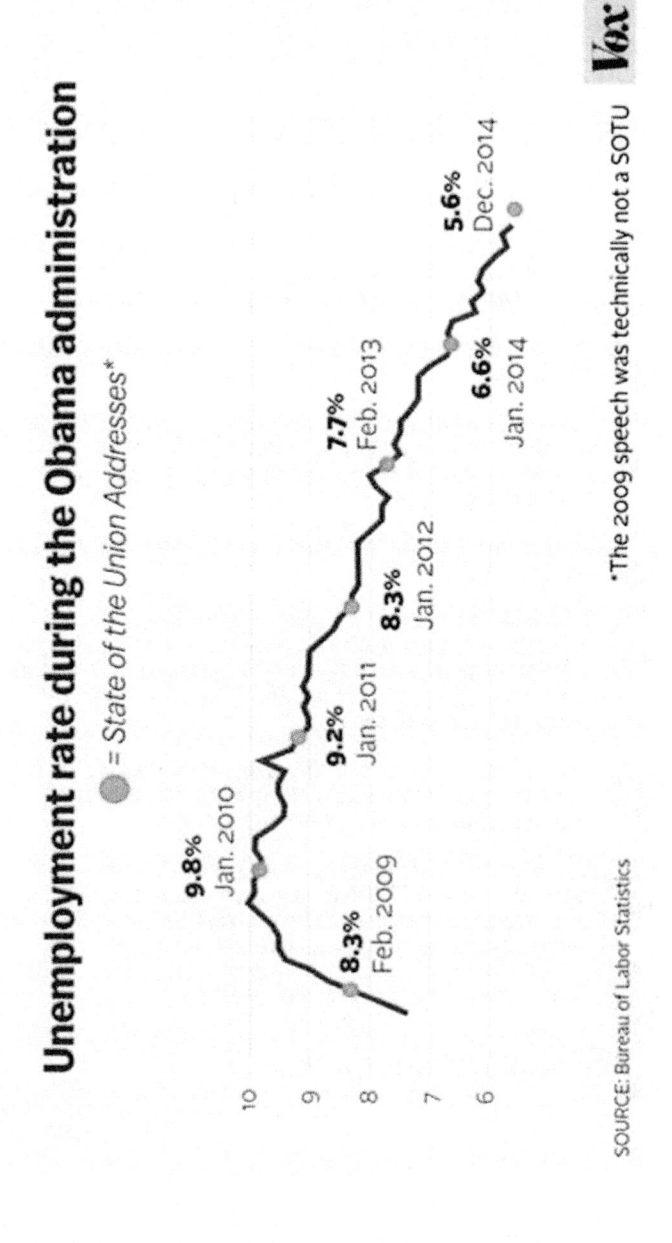

Figure 12: Unemployment Rate Under Pres. Obama

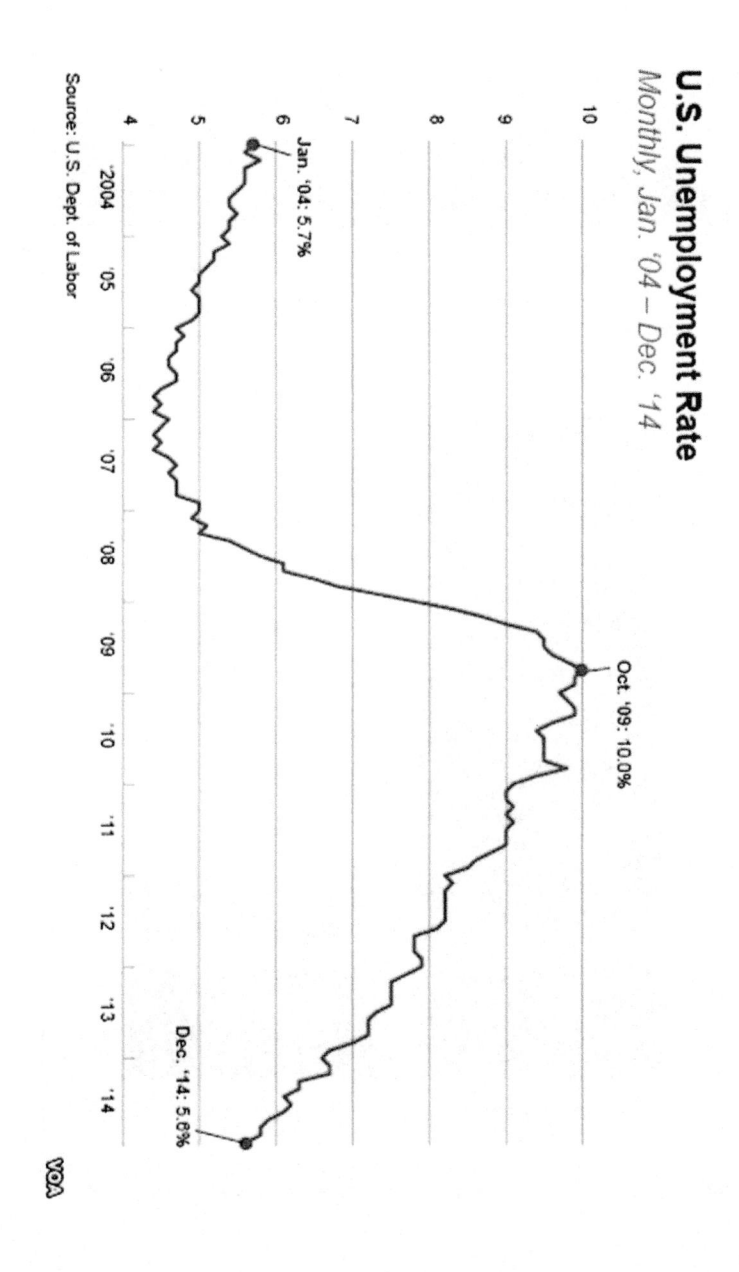

Figure 13: US 10-year Unemployment Rate (04-14)

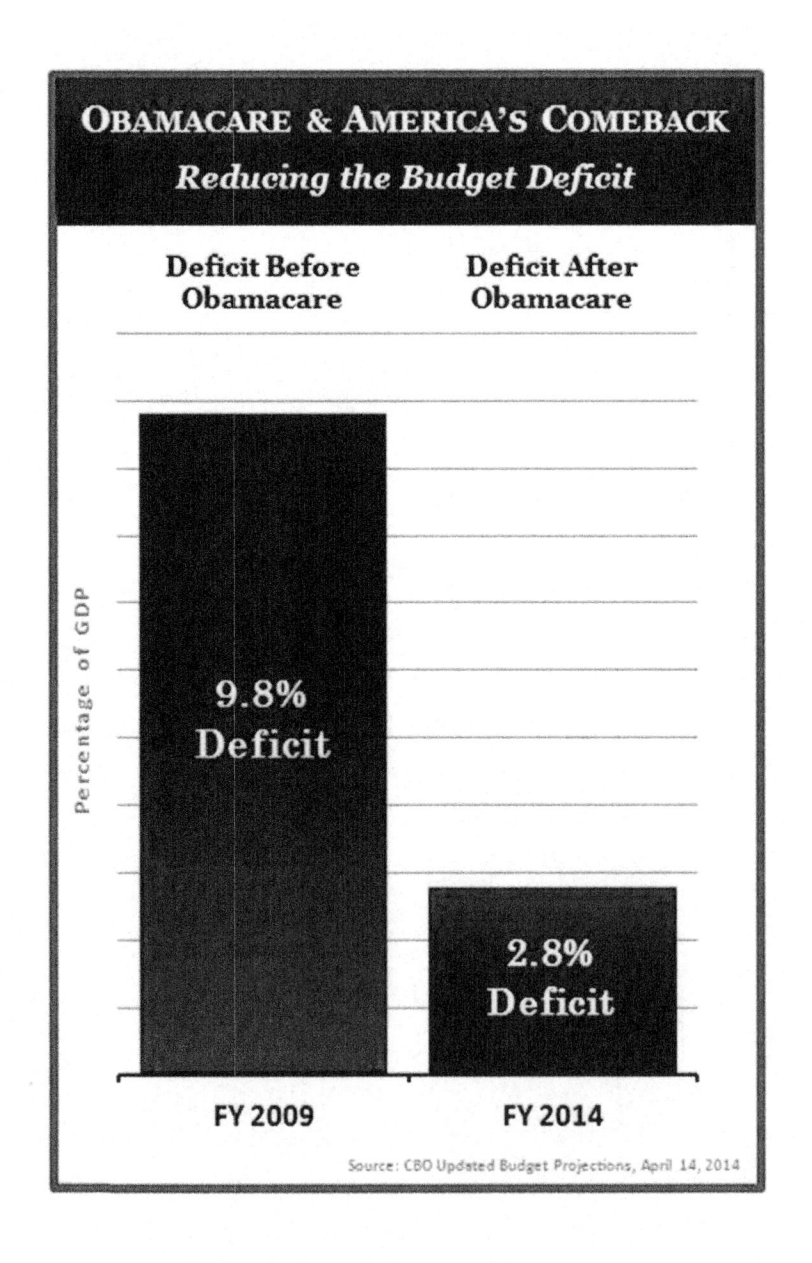

Figure 14: Budget Deficit Reduced under the ACA

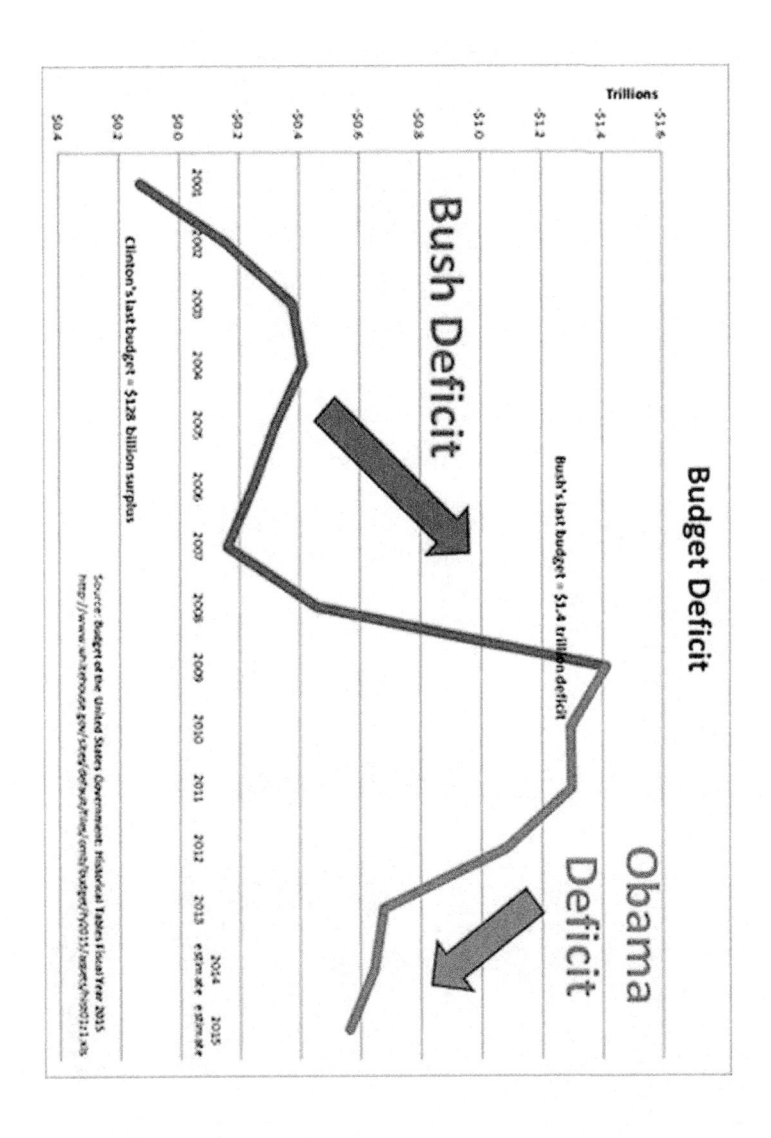

Figure 15: Budget Deficit Comparison. Bush vs. Obama

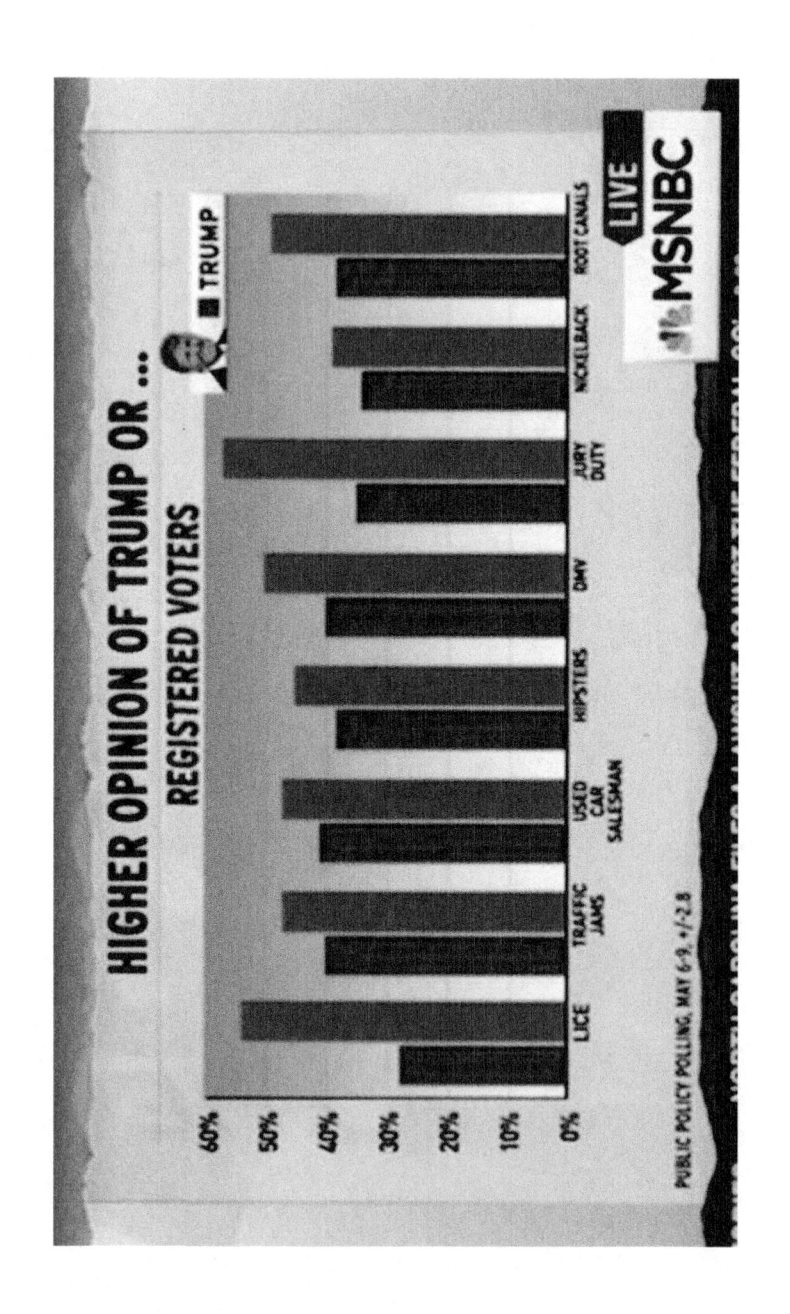

Figure 16: A Higher Opinion of Trump or …?

Sources and Attributions

Image and Graphic Credits:

Figure 1: *The Migration of the "Lost 10 Tribes" of Israel*; The Christian Churches of God; "Abraham's Legacy" (http://abrahams-legacy.org/10-tribes-migration.html) Wade Cox, Editor in Chief, CCG USA; June 13th, 2016; (used by permission)

Figure 2: *Kings of Kallstadt, a Simone Wendel Film*, Projekt Gold/Bernsteiner Film; from *Donald Trump, King of Kallstadt* by Hannelore Crolly; Die Welt, August 24th, 2015; http://www.welt.de/politik/deutschland/article145558110/Donald-Trump-King-of-Kallstadt.html

Figure 3: *Coverage of GOP Candidates, CNN Prime Time Weekly Shows, 8/24/2015 – 9/4/2015*; Daily Kos; "No Thank You CNN" (http://www.dailykos.com/story/2015/12/15/1460469/-NO-THANK-YOU-CNN) Quincy Maxwell, Contributor; June 13th, 2016

Figure 4: Courtesy Pixabay Image Library (https://pixabay.com/) Released under Creative Commons CCO (https://creativecommons.org/publicdomain/zero/1.0/)

Figure 5: *Ibid.*
Figure 6: *Ibid.*
Figure 7: *Ibid.*

Figure 8: Chart: *Obamacare and America's Comeback, The Return of Job Creation*; Daily Kos; "One Simple Chart (Jobs and Obamacare)" (http://www.dailykos.com/story/2014/10/18/1337535/-One-Simple-Chart-Jobs-Obamacare); Jim Oleske, Contributor, October 18th, 2014; Source: U.S. Bureau of Labor Statistics, Total Private Employment, 1-month Change; released under *Freedom of Information Act*; signed July 4th, 1966; President Lyndon B. Johnson; effective July 5th, 1967

Figure : 9 Chart: *Obamacare and America's Comeback, Private Sector Job Creation*; Daily Kos; "One Simple Chart (Jobs and Obamacare)" (http://www.dailykos.com/story/2014/10/18/1337535/-One-Simple-Chart-Jobs-Obamacare); Jim Oleske, Contributor, October 18th, 2014; Source: U.S. Bureau of Labor Statistics, Total Private Employment; released under *Freedom of Information Act*; signed July 4th, 1966; President Lyndon B. Johnson; effective July 5th,

1967

Figure 10: Chart: *Uninsured Rate Among the Nonelderly Population*; The Henry J. Kaiser Family Foundation; (http://kff.org/uninsured/slide/uninsured-rate-among-the-nonelderly-population-1972-2015/); Source: Centers for Disease Control (CDC) and the National Center for Health Statistics (NCHS); released under *Freedom of Information Act*; signed July 4th, 1966; President Lyndon B. Johnson; effective July 5th, 1967

Figure 11: Chart: *10 Things You Now Get to Keep With Obamacare*; Courtesy *Other 98%* (http://other98.com/) Released under Creative Commons Attribution 4.0 International License (http://creativecommons.org/licenses/by/4.0/legalcode)

Figure 12: Chart: *Unemployment Rate During the Obama Administration*; Courtesy *Vox™ Media* (http://www.vox.com/); Source: U.S. Bureau of Labor Statistics; released under *Freedom of Information Act*; signed July 4th, 1966; President Lyndon B. Johnson; effective July 5th, 1967

Figure 13: Chart: *U.S. Unemployment Rate*; Courtesy *VOA – Voice of America English News* (http://www.voanews.com/); Source: U.S. Department of Labor; released under *Freedom of Information Act*; signed July 4th, 1966; President Lyndon B. Johnson; effective July 5th, 1967

Figure 14: Chart: *Obamacare and America's Comeback, Reducing the Budget Deficit*; Daily Kos; "One Simple Chart (Jobs and Obamacare)" (http://www.dailykos.com/story/2014/10/18/1337535/-One-Simple-Chart-Jobs-Obamacare); Jim Oleske, Contributor, October 18th, 2014; Source: Congressional Budget Office (CBO): Updated Budget Projections, April 14th, 2014; released under *Freedom of Information Act*; signed July 4th, 1966; President Lyndon B. Johnson; effective July 5th, 1967

Figure 15: Chart: *Budget Deficit*; Campaign for America's Future; *"Three Updated Charts to Email to your Right Wing Brother-in-Law"* (https://ourfuture.org/20140808/three-updated-charts-to-email-to-your-right-wing-brother-in-law); Dave Johnson, Contributor, August 8th, 2014; Source: Budget of the United States Government; released under *Freedom of Information Act*; signed July 4th, 1966; President Lyndon B. Johnson; effective July 5th, 1967

Figure 16: Chart: *Higher Opinion of Trump Or…*; Addicting

Info The Knowledge You Crave; "Watch Rachel Maddow Troll Trump with a List of Things That Poll Higher Than Him (Video)" (http://addictinginfo.org/2016/05/10/watch-rachel-maddow-troll-trump-with-a-list-of-things-that-poll-higher-than-him-video/); Christian Drake, Contributor, May 10th, 2016; Source: Public Policy Polling, May 6-9, 2016; released through The Rachel Maddow Show, MSNBC, May 9th, 2016

Excerpt Credits:
Excerpts attributed to PolitiFact in Part Two: Donald Trump: *Truth-O-Meter Pants on Fire Rulings* (http://www.politifact.com/truth-o-meter/rulings/pants-fire/); Various contributors; attributed parenthetically within body of text (used by permission).

Quotes by Donald Trump derived from various sources; attributed parenthetically within body of text.

All biblical passages attributed parenthetically within body of text derived from the Holy Bible, King James Version, New International Version, New American Standard Bible, and American Standard Version. Source: *Bible Hub Online Bible Study Suite* (http://biblehub.com/)

Additional references derived from: "21 Attributes of the Antichrist"; Phil Maxwell, Simple Truth Discussion Center at Yuku.com (http://stdebate.yuku.com/topic/1059/21-Attributes-of-the-Antichrist#.V2BPybsrKM8)

All other sources, publically released tweets from GOP Presidential Candidates during 2015-2016 Campaign Season, excerpts, and quotes are attributed parenthetically within body of text.

About The Author

Born in the US to German immigrants, Lawrence Moelhauser is the son of a university language professor and a high school teacher and librarian. He realized early in life that words came easy to him and he began crafting short books in his bedroom in his spare time. His interests eventually took him to film school with aspirations of becoming a screenwriter and film director. A personal setback put his dreams on hold and instead he took a job with the Federal Government, working in Europe, California, and ultimately Washington, D.C. While in the Nation's Capitol, his love of writing was rekindled when he was asked to produce recruiting and sales literature for the Army National Guard. After twenty-two years with the government, he retired from federal service and returned to California to pursue in earnest a career in writing.

Though not overtly religious, Larry is deeply spiritual and spends many quiet hours studying the differences and similarities between world religions, their sacred beliefs and writings, seeking ways to reconcile them in his own heart, and trying to find common ground between them. Larry enjoys serving his fellow human beings and, when not writing or studying, he volunteers his time at the local library and other community events.

The Fourth Beast is his first published non-fiction work.

Printed in Great Britain
by Amazon

42608891R00066